WAKING TO A HAPPY, FULFILLED LIFE

After Sleeping in Negativity

FRANK MIRANDA

WAKING TO A HAPPY, FULFILLED LIFE
AFTER SLEEPING IN NEGATIVITY

iUniverse books may be ordered through booksellers or by contacting:

iUniverse
1663 Liberty Drive
Bloomington, IN 47403
www.iuniverse.com
1-800-Authors (1-800-288-4677)

ISBN: 978-1-4917-7920-0 (sc)
ISBN: 978-1-4917-7919-4 (e)

Library of Congress Control Number: 2015917896

Print information available on the last page.

iUniverse rev. date: 02/05/2016

WAKING
TO A HAPPY,
FULFILLED LIFE

Dear Virginia,

Wish you the best. Hope
You find this work inspirational
In your life!

God Bless!

Frank Muriola

CONTENTS

ACKNOWLEDGMENTS

I would like to thank all the people in my life who have helped me on this journey so I can be more than I am and continue to evolve. Many have supported me both emotionally and spiritually throughout my life. I am very grateful for all the works I have read, listened to, and watched that gave me the knowledge and inspiration to complete this book. Most of my writing was done while I was having coffee at Starbucks. This was a great atmosphere for me to get inspired, focused, and in the zone, and it helped my writing flow from Source. I am also very grateful to the staff of Starbucks—Rihanna, Seda, Isabella, Sasha, Cassie, Victoria, Jessica, Danya, Ashley, Anthony, Ryan, Tom, Nathan, Mike, Chris, MJ, Clemente and Justin. And I add a special thanks to Stephanie and Nicole, whose lovely faces and personalities I've seen and enjoyed every morning for the past five years. The entire staff has always greeted me with respect, friendliness, and warmth. They have been my support as I've written this book. I hope they find this work inspirational in their own lives.

A special thanks to my loving wife, Lisa, who makes our home a welcoming, lovely place for everyone. She takes care of me and our two loving daughters, who I am very proud of. My wife and daughters have been supportive of me writing this book and have watched me as I evolved on this journey. They have been my inspiration to always improve upon myself and grow to be a better person. Without them, I don't know where I would be. Thank you.

INTRODUCTION

After being exposed, in the formative years of my life and beyond, to a negative, ignorant, judgmental, and at times, hostile environment, where prejudice was rampant, I had become that which had influenced me in terms of how I saw life. Then one day, I woke up and said to myself, *This is not right. Why am I so unhappy?* I asked myself why things didn't seem to work out for me. Why didn't I have good relationships with friends and family? Why didn't I have a girlfriend when all my friends had girlfriends or were married? Why wasn't I as successful as I would like to be? Why was I so angry? All these feelings were a result of the environment I had grown up in, and many negative traits had been instilled in my subconscious that I was not aware of. Once I realized where I was in my miserable life and how wrong it was, I started my journey of enlightenment—the journey that would lead me to what I now know to be true.

I turned negativity to positivity; ignorance to intelligence and wisdom; judgment to nonjudgment; prejudice to acceptance and seeing everyone as the same; and anger to love. This has been an immensely enlightening journey that has turned my life around, allowing me to be a good loving, happy, patient, faithful, and productive human being. After conducting years of research in psychology, science, and religion, I have discovered they all correlate with one another, and I am now convinced that we live in a world of all possibilities. This has transformed my life, and I want to share this with all who have had a negative, dysfunctional upbringing. Psychologists say 85 percent of families today are dysfunctional, which was an eye-opener to me. And of course, I was a part of that statistic and didn't even know it.

If you fall into this category, my wish is to take you to a better place in your life so you can be a happy, fulfilled human being. Just imagine having the perfect mate, the career you love, high levels of energy and health, loving relationships, plenty of money to do what you want or to provide for your family, and being at peace. I wrote this book to take you through all the experiences I was exposed to and all the research I conducted in order to illustrate how anyone can change his or her life for the better and evolve to their divine purpose. There were many times in my life where I didn't think things would ever get better and I couldn't get out from under myself, but I now realize that is not the case. *Waking to a Happy, Fulfilled Life* is for you who feel the same way I did and have the courage to take this journey with me, not only for your own good but for the good of all who are around you—and maybe for the world.

PART I

MONEY

CHAPTER I

HOW DID I GET OUT OF MY RUT?

How do you get from wanting to end it all to living in a world of all possibilities? This is my story. I am not a psychologist or a therapist; I'm just an average person who grew up in a negative, judgmental, resentment-filled, prejudiced, and sometimes angry dysfunctional home. Psychologists say 85 percent of all families are dysfunctional. Learning this was a big shocker to me. And I guess I was in one of those families. I'm now an information technology specialist with an educational organization, working in a very professional environment. When I tell my colleagues I grew up in a dysfunctional home, they have trouble understanding because they didn't go through it. How could they understand? Most of them grew up in positive, functional, educated environments; had good relationships with their parents; and always had someone to guide them.

That was not where I came from. I had no guidance from my parents. As a matter of fact, when I turned eighteen, it was like I was the parent and my parents were the children. I remember my mother calling me a bum, saying I was stupid, and telling me, frequently, "Go sit down; you can't do that." It seemed like this was what she'd say every time I wanted to do something.

Another phrase I used to hear was, "They don't want you there." This one would be lobbed at me whenever I wanted to go spend time with friends or even relatives. My parents would always get angry when I asked them for money, and I would hear, "What? Do you think money grows on trees?" or, "If it wasn't for you kids, I'd be walking on money." As a small child I took this to mean that my family's difficult financial situation was entirely my fault. Yes, my mother was a guilt thrower, and I, unfortunately, became a guilt catcher. I have done research on guilt throwers and guilt catchers, and basically, a guilt thrower is someone who is always throwing the blame on someone or something for all the negative events. A guilt catcher is always doing the opposite—receiving the blame and feeling like everything that goes wrong is his or her fault. How did all this make me feel? Well, just awful. I felt inadequate. I believed myself to be a failure. I thought I was to blame when things went wrong. I didn't feel worthy to receive good things and didn't believe I would ever achieve greatness or happiness.

I did, however, wake up and overcome this. And I refuse to be either a guilt thrower or a guilt catcher. To this day I continue to grow, and what I have come to realize is that I *want* to consistently evolve to a higher level. And for me that means doing God's work. Many may think that to do God's work is to preach the Gospel, but it's more than that. God's work is not preaching but setting an example. Be kind, generous, courteous, sympathetic, nonjudgmental, always willing to listen, and always ready to forgive. Forgiveness is huge because when you forgive, you free yourself and you can move on. According to Gautama Buddha (circa 563 BC–438 BC), founder of Buddhism, "Holding on to anger is like grasping a hot coal with the intent of throwing it at someone else; you are the one who gets burned."

So how does God's work fulfill my life and make me happy? Let me explain what this means. Everyone is born with a special talent, and I believe it's a person's responsibility to find out what that talent is, and once it is discovered, a person should live it—making it their purpose or dharma. Living our purposes in life is what will fulfill our lives and bring us true happiness because that is how God made us. God gave us these special abilities, and we all have something to offer. We can contribute to this world in a positive way, and God knows what is right for us. He wants us to live our lives on purpose. He knows we will be happy when we share our special talents with the world, helping others and improving their lives. And this is always different for everyone. When we are in dharma all we need will come to us; whether we're in need of people, money, things, or whatever, it will come. And sometimes it's magical. But the most important thing is to trust and have faith. The more you trust and have faith, the faster and easier your life's purpose will be revealed to you.

Think of people who practice the arts. If they have an idea and become inspired, they will work on it as soon as possible, and they will enjoy the work. It doesn't matter if it is early Sunday morning or Saturday night. They are inspired and motivated to be working on their idea, and time will just fly. And if they are doing this work in conjunction with what the universe has in store for them, it will just flow. The bottom line is that what we all want is to be happy, and happiness is usually different for everyone. Brian Tracy, Canadian entrepreneur, public speaker, author, and personal and professional development trainer has defined happiness as, "the progressive realization of a worthy goal." But it is more than just that; it's our God-given purpose. And this doesn't have to be a religious thing; it can be anything you believe in—energy, universe, some sort of higher intelligence, whatever is right for you. As for me, I used to be very religious, but now I have become very spiritual, which connects me to my source.

I have learned much of what I'm writing about from *The Secret* and *The Magic* by Rhonda Byrne; multiple books by Dr. Wayne Dyer and Deepak Chopra; and *What the Bleep!? Down the Rabbit Hole*, a movie that explains correlations between quantum mechanics, neurobiology, human consciousness, and day-to-day reality. These sources gave me the scientific evidence I needed to believe and pursue my life's purpose. To me, life is truly magical, and I am living proof. I could not otherwise have come from such a negative environment to become the happy, positive, functional, successful individual that I am today. And I couldn't have done so without the knowledge I've found from these resources. I have now achieved things which I'd never thought I could, and I continue to grow and achieve all the things I need and want. As long as a goal is in line with the universe and backed by *good intentions*—I cannot stress this point enough!—it will just flow.

Today I have a loving wife of over twenty-three years, two wonderful children who do very well in school, and a nice home in a good neighborhood. My wife and I both drive new cars, and we have been able to take vacations to Disney World and go on several cruises in the last five years—things I would never have been able to do with the way I used to think. Some of my previous thoughts would be *I can't do that*; *good things don't happen to me*; and *Nothing goes right for me*.

Luckily, God has been with me throughout my entire life, which was always one of my beliefs. But I was still very negative and not living my life like I should. Our lives should be wonderful. We should have loving relationships with our family members and friends and have high levels of health and well-being. And we should always have abundance in our lives. This is the way we were meant to live, not in doubt, worry, anger, hatred, envy, jealously, poverty, or sickness. Dr. Wayne Dyer says our biography becomes our biology, and I believe this to be true. I came to a point in my life when I just knew that something was wrong; I didn't feel right. I didn't know at the time, but now I believe what I was feeling was that I was not living my life on purpose. Living our lives on purpose or dharma brings us true happiness and starts to put us in line with the universe and bring us to our destinies. Following our dharma is always different for everyone, and that is the beauty of God's plan, because it means we can help one another with our unique talents.

CHAPTER 2

ATTRACTING NEGATIVITY

How did I go from wanting to end it all to living in a world of all possibilities and enlightenment? This is my story. I want to share it so it may help others who have gone through similar circumstances. I was born in 1960 in Brooklyn, New York, and lived in a small three-family house with my grandparents, my sister and my parents, and some extended family. My nuclear family lived on the ground floor; there were four rooms—my parents' bedroom, the bedroom I shared with my sister, a dining room, a small kitchen, and one bathroom. To me, our home was big enough. I was small, and since it was my grandparents' home, we also had access to the backyard and the cellar, where my grandfather, who made his own wine, had wine barrels. I only lived there the first five years of my life, and during that time, I spent a lot of time with my grandfather, a happy-go-lucky man, and grandmother, who I don't recall very much of. From what I would later hear, she was very troubled. As far as I can conclude, she had issues such as doubt, worry, and who knows what else. My mother said that my grandmother used to pray that, if she got sick, God would take her in three days. That did happen eventually. She took ill and died in three days. She was only in her sixties, and my grandfather lived to be ninety. After all I have learned, I am sure my mother received much of her doubt, negativity, anger, frustration, and worry from her own mother; to her, everything was a catastrophe.

I look back. (Well actually, I try not to look back, but I'm doing so now because examining my past may help someone else. In fact, likely because of my negative past, I always try to move forward. I like new things and new music. I'm a big believer in the adage "out with the old and in with the new." And I'm always learning and evolving.) At any rate, I look back and see that mine was, overall, not a good environment to grow up in. The problem wasn't the fact that we didn't have money—and we didn't—but it was the negativity and ignorance that always surrounded my immediate family. Many people came from poor backgrounds and did very well because they had good guidance, support, and encouragement from their families. The most important thing for parents to do is nurture high self-esteem in their children, and you can do that regardless of your financial situation. The most important thing is to have mental and spiritual health.

I was growing up in a negative, dysfunctional environment, and I didn't have a clue that was the case. We are born with all we need. We are geniuses, and then life comes along and "de-geniuses" us, according to Dr. Wayne Dyer's work: "The Secrets of an Inspirational (In-Spirit) Life." We are told many different things by many people throughout our lives. Sometimes what we hear is negative, and we start to believe it. And then we attract that into our lives. When we are in the womb, we are given all we need, and we continue to grow from just a fertilized egg to a full infant. Now that's a miracle. God or the universe is always with us, and if we just have faith and just be, all we require will flow to us effortlessly. However, it is very hard to get to this place. Banishing doubt and having faith is something I always found challenging. Many people hate to be challenged and hate change. But I have come to realize that, if you want true happiness and this is what you are focused on, then the changes that you are experiencing are the universe telling you about or showing you the way to a better life. *The universe, science tells us, is dynamic.* So it's always changing, and I feel we should change with it.

I came to this realization when I started my career in information technology and discovered that the more I learn about this ever-changing field, the more there is to learn. Life should also be like this. Most people like to be comfortable and complacent, but when circumstances challenge us at times, it's the universe telling us we need to learn something in order to take us to the next level, so that we can live happy, fulfilled lives. We can ignore this message and live in a space of constant complaining, which just attracts more to complain about, or we can accept what life has given us, learn from it, and move on. A degree of worry always comes with challenging situations or change, and this is something I had consistently found to be very difficult in my life. This is mostly because of my past and because I grew up in a dysfunctional home. My mother worried about everything, and worrying, unfortunately, became another one of the behavoirs I had to overcome. "Gratitude is riches, and complaint is poverty." In the section of *The Magic* that discusses money, Rhonda Byrne said, "Whoever has gratitude (for money), will be given more, and she or he will have an abundance. Whoever does not have gratitude (for money), even what she or he has will be taken from her or him." I have found that reading *The Magic* and *The Secret* (also by Byrne) has helped me tremendously.

You can apply gratitude and faith to any area of your life—health, relationships, money, career, or anything you desire. I chose to talk about money because most people worry about money, and most things we worry about never happen. Worry is a very bad negative trait because we are looking to the future and sending negative signals (vibrations) or frequencies to the universe that indicate things will not work out—something we should never do. Most people do this because this is the way they were taught to think. I am not saying we should never worry about things, but we should be concerned with our situations and have *faith* that all will be fine. This is what I have done with my life to confront all the things I had worried about. I believe God was there to help show me the way, and all worked out.

Always having a purpose gives us strength to move on. I once saw a commercial for New York Presbyterian Hospital that featured our brave veterans and how they often come home from the service and lose their purpose and suffer from post-traumatic stress disorder. These veterans talk about losing the sense of purpose they had during their service and then trying to find it again in civilian life. Unfortunately, most of them don't get the help they need. But the stories of the ones who do find their way again are wonderful and inspiring. Having a purpose in mind is so important; I can't stress it enough. If you don't know what your purpose is, then ask the universe and have faith, and it will be shown to you.

Back to my story—I am a do-it-yourself project. I want to be happy and to live my life to the fullest and on purpose. This is the way to live. The first five years of my life, when I was living in my grandfather's house, was a happy period as far as I know. After that, my parents, sister and myself moved into a six-room apartment on the second floor above a candy store. I was always overweight, and living above the candy store didn't help. Seven years later, when I was in sixth grade, we bought a nice house around the corner. It was a big upgrade compared to where we had been living. It was a two-family house with a finished basement and a backyard. I lived there for a good part of my young life, until I was twenty-four.

These are the places I lived during my formative years and beyond, and where I learned all my negative habits. This is where I picked up my "memes," which comes from the word *memetics*. In the following excerpt from *Excuses Begone! How to Change Lifelong, Self-Defeating Thinking Habits*, Dr. Wayne W. Dyer explains:

> So as the basic unit of genetics is the gene, the basic unit of memetics is the meme (rhymes with "team"). Yet unlike an atom or an election, the meme has no physical properties. According to Richard Broidie, in his work *Virus of the Mind*, it's "a thought belief, or attitude in your mind that can spread to and from other people's minds."
>
> Richard Dawkins, the Oxford biologist who coined the word *meme*, describes the process in his book *The Selfish Gene*. My understanding is that memetics originates from the word *mimic,*

meaning to observe and copy behavior. This behavior is repeated and passed on to others, and on and on the mimicking process goes. The key point is this: *transferring an idea, attitude, or belief to others is done mentally.* We won't find memes by turning up the magnification on any microscope—they pass from mind to mind via hundreds of thousands of imitations. By the age of six or seven, we've all been programmed with an endless inventory of memes that act very much like a virus. They aren't necessarily good or bad; they simply spread easily throughout the population.

I wanted to explain a little about how we are influenced in our lives to behave in certain ways. Unfortunately, most of the time, we behave poorly and don't even realize it.

Excuses Begone! is one of the books that has helped me tremendously; it has propelled me forward in all areas of my life. I would have to say, out of all the books I have read or listened to, this seems to be the best by far. Every time I have doubts and I read this book, it brings me back to believing in myself and having faith in myself and in God. I would recommend this book to anyone who is having difficulty in his or her life.

Many times throughout my life, I have behaved poorly without even realizing it because of the way I was feeling. And I was feeling bad because I was thinking negative thoughts. I believe now that I received most of my negative thoughts from my mother, through memetics. My father had some negative thoughts also, but he was more easygoing than my mother and did whatever my mother told him. She was a very strong-willed woman; unfortunately, she didn't know how to direct her energy to more positive situations, which would have benefitted her and us very much. I don't blame my parents anymore for all the grief they gave me, and they gave me a lot of it growing up. But I do realize now it wasn't done intentionally. I have come to be grateful, and I do forgive them. I am grateful because it sent me on this never-ending journey of evolution for myself, and I forgive them because it sets me free.

CHAPTER 3

HOW I ATTRACTED MONEY INTO MY LIFE

I have attracted many good things into my life, and I've attracted many bad things as well, without knowing I was the one doing it. I know now that I was the one attracting everything into my life, just as all people attract everything into their own lives. Winston Churchill said, "We create our universe as we go along." So whatever our thoughts focus on is what we bring into our lives. If we want to attract money, we have to focus on wealth, have faith, and banish all the doubt. I am starting with money because it's typically the one thing most people think about and want. However, this applies to everything—wealth, health, relationships, or anything else in your life.

My background was one of lack. My family didn't have many material things, and we didn't seem to have good relationships either. My mother was always putting down my father—and everyone else, for that matter. Wherever we lived, she always found a neighbor to fight with. It wasn't that she was a bad person; she just didn't know how to cope. She was a very frustrated woman who worried about everything, thought everyone was out to get her in a bad way, and focused on what she did not have and was missing in her life. So there was a great deal of lack in my life and a lot of misdirection of feelings and emotions, and of course I became a product of my environment. Luckily, my father was more laid-back, which kept some sanity in our family. But he too had many negative traits. He also did not seem to have much motivation when it came to making a better life for our family. It was my mother who eventually pushed him into trying to find a better job, which he did. His new job had better opportunities, and that gave us a better life. We could buy a home and our necessities. There wasn't too much left over for luxuries, but we got through.

The reason some people are more successful than others is related to upbringing. If people grow up with wealth and abundance, then that is what they are focused on, and that becomes part of their lives. When people are brought up with lack and negativity, then that is what they are focused on, and that is what they bring into their lives. Lack and negativity became part of my life, and I thought that was the way it should be, because that was all I had been exposed to. That is how my neural network was formed in my brain. I have done some research, and from what I understand, our neural networks are formed by how we think, and then it forms our neurons in our brain. So our neurons are formed depending on how we think, and this is how we continue our thinking patterns, whether positive or negative.

I am not saying that all people brought up in lack are unsuccessful; I believe now that success depends on how negative or positive a person's environment was and what kind of support system he or she had. Studies have found that families who are welfare recipients sometimes have children who become welfare recipients because the talk around the dinner table is about receiving welfare, and that is all they know. These patterns will continue to happen until we start to think differently, and then things will begin to change. According to quantum physics, as we change the way we look at things, those things start to change. This was a big eye-opener for me, and once I understood this concept, my life changed tremendously.

Once we were living above the candy store, I started to gain a lot of weight. My mother, like many Italian mothers who feed their sons until they're overweight, just kept feeding me. And I did like my sweets.

Luckily, there was enough money for food, but we did not have many extras. One year for Christmas, my parents gave my sister and I rewrapped gifts—toys we already had. I was still too young to realize the difference, but all my relatives, with the exception of one or two, were much better off than us financially, and I had a lot of relatives. That is where the jealousy and resentment started. My mother was always saying that my father wasn't making enough money and that, if it weren't for us kids (my sister and I), she would be walking on money. Again more negativity poured into my head, building my neural net into the thinking I was growing up with; in essence, I had believed that bad circumstances were my fault and I wasn't good enough.

Then when I was in sixth grade, my parents were finally able to afford a two-family home with a finished basement and a small yard. The second floor had six rooms, five of which we rented out and one we kept as a spare room. Having a finished basement was very modern at the time, and my sister and I just loved living there. It was so much better than anything we'd had and what we'd grown accustomed to. It was a miracle that my parents were able to afford this house, and I was very happy at the time. I was probably very grateful too, but I didn't realize that. We rented the upstairs apartment to three elderly people. They were very quiet, and my mother liked it that way. My mother did not get along with many people because she was very judgmental and controlling—two very bad attributes we must overcome in order to live happy, fulfilled lives.

Something very interesting about this house my parents purchased was that we almost did not buy it because it was a little out of our price range, and someone else had already been in contract to buy it. When we were looking for a house, we did look at a couple of houses. But when we saw the house we finally bought, my sister and I fell in love with it. Even though at the time we thought it was out of reach, my sister and I poured all our thoughts and energy into the house. Following the law of attraction, which states, "Whatever we think about, we create or bring into our lives," we brought this house into our lives. The law of attraction is in direct correlation with the laws of quantum mechanics. You see, our thoughts create the particles that create the atoms and electrons that create the molecules that form our universe. This is an oversimplified explanation, but it is somewhat accurate. If you want further detail, you can always research quantum physics, or you can watch *What the Bleep!? Down the Rabbit Hole*. This film will give you a better understanding of and enlighten you as to our true nature. It's all about the science, which I will try to explain in more detail later.

After my parents had purchased the house that my sister and I fell in love with, I was in sixth grade, and my life seemed normal to me. My parents provided for us, and I continued my elementary education. I later went on to attend high school and then college.

My parents gave me a hard time about college. My mother always used to say, "Tell me something. What are you going to do with this college education?" And I would say, "Get a job." My parents didn't believe in college. They wouldn't let my sister attend. They thought she would get married, have children, and stay home. Well, of course they were wrong. My sister got married and then divorced and then married a second time, only to get divorced again. She never had children and, unfortunately, never had a very successful career. She did work and was able to buy a home. But going to college would have opened up more possibilities for her.

At one point when my mother was still alive, my sister told her that she might have a date. "Who would want to go out with you?" my mother responded.

When my sister told me this, I was shocked. But my mother acted this way when she was in the last years of her life and taking a lot of medication, including antidepressants and antisuicidal medications. All I could think was, *How could a parent speak to her child like this?* I have two beautiful daughters, and I could not see myself speaking to them in a derogatory manner. My daughters are teenagers now, and sometimes they are difficult, like most teenagers. And believe me, some days are more difficult than others. But I am always there for them. I think back to when I was a teenager and how difficult that period of my life was for me. I can only imagine what they are going through. A parent is supposed to nurture high levels of self-esteem in his or her children and always be supportive. Parents should never demoralize their children.

While I was going to college in the early '80s, I could not see an end—I couldn't envision getting a job and having a career. There was no way I could imagine this becoming a reality because no one in my family had ever gone to college; I had no idea what pursuing that goal and finishing it looked like. I felt I could not be successful due to all the negativity that had been put into my head over the years. This of course gave me low self-esteem. I lacked confidence and was plagued by the belief that I was not good enough. I really never excelled at anything, because I didn't think I could. When I was in elementary school and my mother was helping me with my homework, she would call me stupid when I got something wrong. She was trying to be funny, and her thinking was that, if she called me stupid, I would try harder. But that doesn't work. If you tell your child, "You never clean up your room," then behold, the child will never clean his or her room. If a child has been told repeatedly by his or her parent or another authority figure that he or she is a person who doesn't clean, that child won't clean. We must be sure to always keep what we say to our children or anyone else who sees us as an authority figure positive or constructive.

I finally graduated from a two-year college in four years because I was working to help support myself. When I started college, I was not working. I just wanted to focus on my studies for two years and finish, graduate, and start working. I had a good car, which was paid for, and enough money in the bank to support myself while I was going to college. I asked my parents to pay my tuition. It was a community college and very inexpensive at the time, but my parents were adamant then they would not pay the tuition unless I had a job. Of course, I could not see the reasoning behind this stipulation. After all, I was doing very well. I was receiving As and Bs in all my classes, and I did not have to ask them for any spending money. After much aggravation, I got a job working Monday through Friday from seven to eleven in the evening, and all my grades fell.

My parents were never logical, or what I used to think was logical. It wasn't that they didn't have the money; *it was just that they were trapped in their own negative neural patterns*. They were very negative and ignorant. They were not stupid; I don't believe anyone is stupid. They just lacked knowledge and the willingness to open their minds to new ideas. That, combined with negativity, can hold anyone back from achieving his or her goals or greatness.

While going to college I worked at United Parcel Service. I started off unloading trucks. Later I became a part-time supervisor. I did like the job at the time and was going to pursue a career at the company, but then I had a change of heart and started looking for a career in my field. After a long search, I found a job at a small firm doing CAD (computer-aided design) work. It was okay, and I enjoyed working in my field. I wasn't making a lot of money, but it was a job with benefits.

About a year later, I moved out of my parent's house to be closer to work. Then a month later, the company had a layoff and let go over twenty employees. I was one of them. I was devastated. I did not dare tell my parents. I knew they would only yell at me and tell me how I was ruining their lives. I could just hear them saying that I was no good at anything and knew they'd figure out a way to make it all my fault. I could not go to them for help, so I went to the library and brushed up on my computer skills. I had several interviews, and after a couple of weeks, I received a position as a test technician. It paid less money than I'd previously been making, but it was a job with benefits. I did not stop looking though. I knew this job wasn't for me. It just had to hold me over until I found something better. Luckily, my continued search paid off, and I found a better position a couple of months later, with a 30 percent increase in salary. I was very excited and relieved that I had finally found a good position with benefits and room for advancement.

Deep down, I knew God was looking out for me. Even though I had my doubts, my faith prevailed. Back when I'd been laid off, one of my coworkers, who'd also been let go, had told me she knew God would take care of me because I was so religious. And she was right. It had all worked out; this was another miracle in my life I was very thankful for.

A few months later, my parents moved closer to where I was living, and I moved back in with them. It wasn't that I couldn't afford to live on my own; with my increased salary, I was fine. It was the loneliness, which I'll talk about in another section on relationships, that motivated me to move back in with them. I also figured I could save some money. Now I know that move was a big mistake, as I did not need any more of my parents' influence in my life.

At this time, I was in my midtwenties and working at my new position. I even started going back to school to get my bachelor's degree. I found school very difficult at this time because of other issues I was dealing with in my life. I will speak later about these issues and about how I overcame them. I even tried to switch my curriculum to an easier one. School just wasn't for me at the time. I was not ready for it. My life was missing good relationships with other people and with myself. I was really lost.

A good friend of mine gave me a set of tapes called *The Psychology of Achievement* by Brian Tracy. I listened to the tapes over and over again, and I started thinking differently and becoming happier. I started setting goals, and at the time, I felt that I should pursue a career in sales. I was working for a defense contractor, and the workflow had stopped. Many people were leaving, and it was only a matter of time before the company closed. I went on many interviews and received a position in sales, which only lasted several months. During that time, I found that sales was not for me. Unfortunately, I found myself out of work again. However, I was living at home with my parents, so at least I didn't have to worry about rent or too many bills. A couple of months later, I received a job offer. I hated the position because of my would-be boss, the work, and the hours. But I needed a job, so I accepted the offer.

At the time, the economy was not doing well. That was especially true for the government defense industry, which was the sector I was working in at the time. That job didn't go well either. The company had a major reduction in work and had to let many employees go. I was one of them.

Back to the job search I went. A month later I was working in the city as a consultant. The pay was good, but the job didn't come with benefits or overtime. I was able to pay my bills, but that was all. It was my first job in the city, and it was very exciting at first. The location was great. I was working on Park Ave in Manhattan. However, after a few months, commuting two hours each way started to wear me down. I was spending too much money on medical benefits and commuting, so I continued to look for a better position.

I found one at Penn Plaza, right where the railroad stopped in the city. The office was upstairs. It was a forty-hour-a-week job with benefits and a lot of overtime. The money started flowing in, which was great. But once again, the commute and all the extra hours were wearing on me. My day started at four thirty in the morning, and I'd get home anywhere from six to seven and sometimes later. It was a very long, tiring day. All I thought about all day was the commute and how it was depriving me of time—time I could be doing other things.

What I realize now is that I was using most of my energy to focus on how terrible my commute was, and that—a terrible commute—was exactly what the universe was giving back to me. (Remember that *the law of attraction* states that whatever we focus on expands and becomes our reality.) Even though I still wanted a career out of the city, my thoughts were keeping me there. I would go to a church sometimes during lunch. I would light a candle and say a prayer that I would find a career out of the city. Where I wanted to be is what I should have been focusing on instead of the commute. Deep down, I always felt and believed God was watching over me (again the law of attraction comes into play). All I needed was more faith.

At this time, I was in my early thirties and was engaged to get married. Two months before my wedding, the firm I was working for decided to reduce its workforce and let many people, including me, go. Again I found myself out of work. I was devastated. It was two months before my wedding. It was supposed to be a happy time in my life. I was supposed to be caught up in the excitement of planning a wedding and all the joy that goes with it. We were so close to the wedding date, and all the down payments had been made. So we went through with it. We felt calling the wedding off didn't make sense. So every day we continued to plan, and I frantically searched for a new job. I prayed that I would find something, but nothing was transpiring. I worried. Who would hire me when, in a couple of months, I had to take three weeks off for my honeymoon? But I knew deep down and had faith that it would all work out.

But God had a plan for me—a plan I couldn't have imagined. During the time I was out of work, my fiancée had a lawsuit pending. I knew about it, but of course it had slipped my mind because of all the other things going on. Her case went to trial, and she asked if I would go with her. Since I was out of work, I did attend. I had only been at my previous job for two years, and I had been saving my time off for the honeymoon, which of course didn't matter now. If I had been working, I would not have been able to take time off to go to the trial. Was my being there part of God's plan, or was it just coincidence? Who's to say for sure? I believe there are no coincidences, just the universe helping us along when we need it. After it was all over, my fiancée won the lawsuit, and the settlement was much more than I would have earned in two months. As a matter of fact, it was over a year's pay for me at the time. The way all the events had led up to this was very interesting. Whether or not my being at the trial was key, the outcome was very positive. This is why we must have faith, accept the circumstances we find ourselves in, keep ourselves open, and surrender to the possibilities.

The wedding was magical for me. We even received many monetary gifts, which further improved our financial situation.

From the time of the bachelor party to the rehearsal dinner to the wedding and the entire honeymoon, I was elated. I did not think about my work situation at all. It was magical, as if God had removed all the negative thoughts and anxiety from me so I could enjoy one of the happiest times of my life. I was filled with gratitude. My normal MO would have been to focus on not having a job. For me the opportunity to completely enjoy the moment without focusing on worries was a miracle.

When my wife and I got back from our honeymoon, I continued to look for a job and found one in a week. It was a good position, but neither the company nor the pay was great. I continued to look, and five months later, I found a great position consulting at the Trade Center in downtown Manhattan. The location was fantastic, and so was the pay. Even some of my coworkers were great. I loved working there, even though the commute was long.

A year later, my wife and I were able to save a lot of money and buy a very nice, move-in-condition home with four bedrooms and three baths. It was a step up from our small, one-bedroom apartment. We even had money to do some slight improvements and buy all the furniture we needed. It was great for a while, and we were enjoying ourselves with our family and friends and our new home. Then our first daughter came, and life got rough again. My wife wanted to stay home with the baby, but she had the job with benefits, and I did not, since I was consulting. My parents and my wife's mom were watching my daughter for the first year, which was not working out well. It was too much for them.

Meanwhile, at my place of employment, my boss told me I needed to go back to school to enhance my skills if I wanted to continue working there. With reluctance, I did. I went, hoping that with my continued education, I would receive a permanent position with benefits. I was taking night classes, one class a semester, at New York Institute of Technology (NYIT), on track to receive my bachelor's degree. Working in the city, going to school, completing all the homework, and having a baby at home made for a very difficult time. What's more, taking the classes didn't seem to make a difference when it came to me obtaining a full-time position. So I started a new job search, which I conducted very slowly. This went on for a couple of years, and in the meantime, I took some good classes to enhance my technical skills. This enabled me to receive a position at Lockheed Martin, where I did support work for the Federal Aviation Administration. The job had benefits and tuition reimbursement, both of which I needed desperately, especially since I was paying out-of-pocket for school. It was not a great position, but the hands-on experience was extremely valuable.

All this enabled my wife to quit her job and stay home with our daughter. She also watched another child for some extra money. Unfortunately, it wasn't enough. We were fortunate to have money in the bank, but every week I was taking money out just to make ends meet. It was a very difficult time financially. Going out to dinner at a fast-food restaurant was a big event at the time; it was awful. We went from living well, paying all our bills with ease, saving a lot of money, and going out to eat both in the city and locally to just getting by.

At my new job, I had an opportunity to change schools and my course of study. I started working toward certification as a Novell Certified Engineer. I completed the coursework in a little over a year and then took some Microsoft classes. My employer paid for all these classes, which I was very grateful for. It was a lot of extra work on my part. I remember sometimes getting home from school after ten. My daughter would get up in the middle of the night, as that's what babies do. Then I would go to work the next day at six thirty. I put in long days between work and school, and I was also spending a lot of time on homework and studying. Looking back, I don't know how I did it. I believe the motivation was providing for my family, and with God's help, I persevered. Amid all this, my second daughter was born.

During this time period, money was really tight. Our family was struggling, and we didn't receive much support from anyone, not even our own families. They just were not capable of helping us either financially or with watching our children.

Then my wife saw an ad in the paper for a position in my field. The work was similar to what I was doing for my present employer but with an educational organization. I sent in a résumé and had an initial interview. Since it was a civil service position, I needed to take a test. After two tests, five interviews, and almost two years, I received an offer. I had to turn it down at first because the pay was less than I was earning. I really wanted this position; I knew it was for me. I wrote a letter thanking the organization and explaining that I wanted to work for an educational organization. My parents didn't believe in education, and having seen what a good education could mean, I had become a huge believer in it. Despite the long process and my initial disappointment over the salary, I continued to think about this and had faith. Two months later, I received another offer, this one comparable to my salary. I was ecstatic. This position had everything I was looking for—the opportunity for advancement working in my field, better benefits than I'd had at my previous job, more time off to spend with my family, and a feeling of belonging.

With enthusiasm, I accepted the position. On my first day, I was working on a new installation—working overtime and being compensated for it. I was always learning new things, I had the opportunity to work many extra hours, and I enjoyed my coworkers. I had finally obtained what I needed to provide for my family, who it had always been about. I am a husband and father, and I want to provide for my family. The course of events that led me to this place was in line with the law of attraction. I'd always had, and still do have, faith in God. I even went for spiritual counseling when I was going through difficult times. Monsignor Tom Hartman, who had a television show called *Telecare* and married my wife and I, was very helpful. Through him, I was able to put things into perspective.

I need to mention that I was still employed at the Trade Center in 1993 when it was bombed. Even though it was a scary experience, I still wanted to work there. It was a great place to work, and I wanted to stay. But God knew there was something better for me. I believe I would have been out of the city sooner if my thoughts were more in line with my desires and not my fears or the things I didn't want to happen, which I thought about a lot. I was too busy focusing on things like how much I hated my commute or the money issues or comparing myself with everyone else. This only brought more of that negativity into my life. Now I know what I should *always* focus on—what I want, not what I don't want. If I had stayed in the city, I most likely would have stayed at the Trade Center. Who knows what would have happened to me on 9/11? I believe God had different plans for me.

In *The Secret*, which I mentioned earlier, Byrne says that we are the "don't want generation" because we focus more on what we don't want and not on what we do want. We should always be aware of where our thoughts are. And when things don't work out the way we want, we might consider that it's the universe pointing us in a different direction. Be aware of what we ask for and how, the more we focus on that, the closer we get to it. Sometimes life gives us challenges in order to teach us the lessons that will allow us to obtain our desires. We need to accept the situation we are in, which is something I always have to remind myself. I have come to realize that the more I focus on a negative situation, by the law of attraction, the more I bring that negative situation to my life. In other words, I am rehashing exactly what I don't want over and over, not realizing that by doing so, I'm bringing more of it into my life. When we accept our circumstances, I believe doing so releases us so we can move forward, and solutions start to appear.

For instance, when I was working at the Trade Center, my employer told me I needed to go back to school. At first, I resisted; I was married and had children, and I didn't want to consider going back to school. Then I accepted it. And going to school set in motion a chain of events that would redirect the course of my journey, enabling the universe to rearrange people, places, and things. This new course enabled me to find my next position and work outside the city. There, at my employer's suggestion, I changed my course of study to one that would most benefit both of us. These new studies helped me excel at my position. I continued to look for a better position, and the interview process with my present employer showed me the organization was a perfect match for me. All this matched up exactly with my desires. I focused and prayed to receive a position out of the city, somewhere close to home that offered benefits and a lot of time off. And that is what I had received. It felt like a miracle, and I was so grateful. This was all in line with the *law of attraction*, which *The Secret* explains is like the law of gravity; it exists, it's precise; and it works every time when we are on the matching frequency with our desires. I will try my best to explain this later, because we should live our lives in alignment with the law of attraction.

If you want to attract money into your life, you need to give from a full heart. Give without any strings attached. This means not expecting anything in return and giving with only the intention of giving and seeing others happy because of it. I would like to share a story of what happened to me when I needed money to give my daughter a sweet-sixteen birthday party. That same year, I wanted to throw a surprise birthday party for my wife.

I would go to Starbucks every morning and sit, have coffee, and read. After a while, I had met some other customers, and we became friendly. We would sit and talk together. At one point, a homeless man was coming in every day. He would sit with our group, and we would take turns buying him coffee and breakfast. At first I was reluctant to buy him breakfast. It seemed like homeless people often just wanted handouts, and it became an ongoing process that never changed. I thought we would be consistently supporting him. After seeing everyone buying him breakfast, I remembered what Jesus said in the Bible about what you should do when you see someone in need and how what you do to them is like doing it to Jesus.

Some would say that there are people who just want to take advantage of others, but the way I see it now is that I did the right thing and gave from a full heart, expecting nothing in return. What others do with what we give them is up to them, and the universe will give them back what they put out. A well known quote by Albert Einstein is, "The most important decision we make is whether we believe we live in a friendly or hostile universe." We must decide what kind of universe we live in—whether it is a friendly universe or a hostile universe—and what we decide is what we will attract into our lives. If I give and someone takes advantage of the situation, then I know I did the right thing and they did the wrong thing, and karma will take care of all that.

Life is all about helping one another. I now believe that is part of the reason we are here. My thought process changed, and I started buying breakfast for the homeless man, coffee or an egg on a roll. And from time to time, I gave him money for transportation to see a doctor. The way I looked at it was I had an opportunity to help someone. Then I discovered that he was trying to get back on his feet. It's strange how things start to change when we change. While this was going on, I started working a lot of overtime at work and had many challenging projects. The homeless man, meanwhile, was able to get himself into a semi-trailer driving school. After a few months, he graduated, found a job, and was able to reconnect with his family. I was able to have both parties in a catering hall and was able to surprise my wife. What a wonderful story of how we were able to get someone who was homeless but with goals and potential to be a self-supporting, productive human being. This was huge, and all that happened because I believed in the law of attraction, which in this case meant giving without expecting anything in return. I had helped someone, and whatever I spent on him came back over a hundredfold. This is how the universe works.

In summary, going with the flow of the universe and trying not to fight but rather accepting the circumstances in our lives is always a good idea. Acceptance will send us on journeys toward better places, and our thinking will start to change. This will put us on a different frequency, and we will attract the same to us. Whatever our desires are, we must ask for them, send a request to the universe or God or whatever you believe in, and have faith. I have always found, when the time and circumstances are right, everything just flows so well. No matter what's going on in our lives, as long as we have faith, keep ourselves open to the possibilities, stay focused on what we want, and remain flexible in terms of what's coming to us, all will work out well.

PART II

RELATIONSHIPS

CHAPTER 4

SURVIVING NEGATIVE INFLUENCES

Having grown up in a dysfunctional environment, I have always found relationships challenging. At a young age, I didn't realize anything was wrong because, in my world, my circumstances all seemed normal. We all become a product of our environment, and we end up repeating whatever it is that makes up all we know. As I mentioned earlier, my mother would always find someone to fight with. No matter where we lived, she found someone. She always looked mad, and she told us on many occasions that people often told her that. I believe that, deep down, she was not happy with her life. She thought people were either out to get her or jealous of her. I don't know what people could have been jealous of because we did not have much. She was frustrated with her life. She was a guilt thrower and sometimes a guilt catcher as I had stated earlier, which she most likely received from her mother. There are guilt throwers, people who are always making anything that goes wrong someone else's fault, and guilt catchers, those who are constantly receiving the blame. At some point, I became the same—a guilt thrower and a guilt catcher.

I had many issues while I was growing up. My mother babied me and smothered me, and I was like her in many ways. I don't believe I had issues because my mother babied or smothered me with love. I believe it was all her negative traits, and my father wasn't much help. It wasn't that my parents were bad people. They were not. They just didn't have the tools we have now to cope with life. They were stuck in the 1940s and never progressed with the times. For instance, they felt all the newer music was terrible noise, and now we call it classic rock; go figure. The importance of continuing to grow with the times and to evolve is something I learned from observing my life. I do like a lot of the new music my children listen to. I enjoy new things and changing with the times because it means I am growing with society, hopefully to a better place.

My father also had many negative traits. He wasn't very motivated to better himself, and he was very laid-back. He would come home every night from work, eat dinner, help clean up after dinner, and then watch TV the rest of the night. At first my mother didn't work. Then as my sister and I got older, she started working. But nothing changed. That was the old way of thinking. The men worked, and the women stayed home, tending to the home and children. When my mother started working, that's when my father should have started helping more. But nothing changed. However, we made it through. It wasn't the greatest environment, but it wasn't the worst either. With that said, I have to say there is nothing in my childhood that I miss; for me, it was that bad. When I got married and finally moved out, I felt free. It was great.

At one point in my life, I realized I wasn't happy. I was miserable. And like my mom, I would always find someone to fight with. I didn't think that people were witches like my mother had, but I did think people hated me or wanted to use me or were jealous of me. Sounds like my mother, doesn't it? Of course, we become product of our environments. Recall memetics and our tendency to emulate everything we receive from other people, especially our parents or any authority figure.

With so much negativity around me, I had developed many issues with my own relationships. I was negative, doubtful, and had a lot of anger issues. I was also judgmental, jealous, and filled with envy. I guess I was always looking for the bad—glass half-empty kind of stuff. I felt inadequate. My parents made me feel this way when they would say things like, "You can't do that," or, my mother's favorite expression, "Go sit down," which meant, don't even try. My parents gave me no encouragement, inspiration, financial or emotional support, or direction as to how I should live my life. They were on autopilot; they just lived day to day with no plan, always looking back, and constantly blaming their situation on someone or something else—the government, the economy, groups of people, individuals, and even me and my sister. Since that was their focus of attention, they kept attracting the same situations into their lives. Instead of blaming others, they should have focused on bettering themselves. We need to take responsibility for our lives instead of blaming, because when we place blame, we look to the past and what cannot be undone. But when we take responsibility, we look to the future and what can be changed.

This correlates directly with the law of attraction. What we focus on expands. Just like the law of gravity—which states that the larger the object, the more force of gravity it has, and the closer we get to an object, the faster we move toward it—the law of attraction works according to "size" and proximity. The more we focus on our desires, the stronger the attraction becomes. And if others are also focused on the same things, the force only gets more powerful, bringing our desires closer to us at an accelerated rate.

I always try to give my wife and children encouragement and any inspiration I can with whatever they do. I tell them, "You don't know unless you try"—something I remind myself of all the time. Maintaining this outlook is a battle, but it does get easier as we become more and more aware of our negative thoughts.

How did I overcome all this? Luckily, I always had faith in God, and yes, I did go to church and pray a lot. I can't say enough about the power of God in our lives. It doesn't matter what religion you identify with or believe in, as long as you answer to a higher calling, it will help with whatever you are going through. Religion or spiritually can be combined with therapy or other methods to overcome many of life's negative situations. I used to be very religious, but now I am very spiritual. As far as therapy, I do believe it can help in many situations. What I have come to realize is that therapy helps us start to think differently. When we start to see life differently, our world starts to change. As quantum physicists explain, when we start to look at things differently, then those things start to change.

For all this to work, we must have faith in ourselves and in God or the universe. Many researchers have studied the intercepting points between science and religion. If you watch *What the Bleep?! Down the Rabbit Hole*, you will see the correlation between science and spirituality. The two work hand in hand. Max Planck, a German theoretical physicist who originated quantum theory, which won him the Nobel Prize in physics in 1918, stated, "Anybody who has been seriously engaged in scientific work of any kind realizes that over the entrance to the gates of the temple of science are written the words: 'Ye must have faith.'"

When I first read this and saw *Down the Rabbit Hole*, life started to take on new meaning for me. What an eye-opener. Having faith in our own lives, just like having faith in science, is very important. The government and modern day educators took religion out of our public schools, a decision I personally don't agree with. If we believe that God created all things, then when we teach about science and the atoms, protons, electrons, and everything that goes with that, then we are teaching about God's creations, are we not?

CHAPTER 5

NEGATIVE EMOTIONS

There are several traits I want to speak about. The first is negativity. I'll talk about how it affected me and how I overcame it. A negative outlook is one of the worst outlooks a person could have. In my opinion and from what experience has taught me, negativity just keeps us stuck in our situations. Going through life with this attitude is one of the most awful ways to live. I found if we are constantly negative, people don't want to be with us, we can't have good intimate relationships, everything seems to go wrong day after day, and we are always looking for the bad. I was a very negative person, a habit I most likely picked up from my parents. My parents used to advise me not to believe everything I heard. This is a valid point; we should take most of what we hear with a grain of salt. But we should also keep an open mind. So whatever kind of universe we believe we live in, friendly or hostile, our beliefs will bring into our lives whatever we deeply believe.

It's amazing how long I was a negative person. Even when things were going well, I would start to think, *This can't last*. That was my negative traits coming out. I would react very negatively to bad situations, which was how my parents would react to similar situations—like it was the end of the world. Our reactions are what count when something happens in our lives. Instead of thinking, *This is the end of the world*—and in most cases, that is not so—we must look for the challenge in the situation and what we can learn from it. I believe that when we ask God or the universe for something we are sent lessons so that we can learn what we need to learn in order to achieve our goals. Recall the time I lost my job two months before my wedding, I took it negatively, and of course, that was a negative event. Even though I was upset, everything worked out. Maybe if I had still been working twelve- to fourteen-hour days in the city, I could not have done all the prep that was needed for the wedding. My work schedule before I was laid off didn't leave much time for anything else.

As I mentioned, my wife's lawsuit settlement helped us tremendously. Another interesting thing happened during that time period. We were looking for an apartment, and we needed one month's rent, a broker's fee, and a security deposit, which was equal to three months' rent. One night, I had a dream that I was circling numbers on a lotto ticket. The dream was quick and a little fuzzy so I didn't remember the actual numbers, just circling them. It was a special lottery called Leap Year Lotto since it was a Leap Year and the jackpot was $25,000,000. Given my situation, I felt it was God sending me a message and of course I listened. The next chance I got I played five-dollar quick pick and got five out of six numbers, which covered the entire apartment's fees. This was very strange given all the circumstances—I was out of work, getting married, needed money for our apartment, a special lottery and a dream, a message from the Universe. I always feel God is looking out for me, and I believe He is.

Were these coincidences or is there an order to the universe? I found a quote online by David Richo, which is from his book, *The Power of Coincidence: How Life Shows Us What We Need to Know*. "We do not create our destiny; we participate in its unfolding. Synchronicity works as a catalyst toward the working out of that destiny," Richo writes. I believe now that there are no coincidences, just laws of the cosmos. And as Richo states in the title of his book, "Life shows us what we need to know."

We must be aware of what we ask for; after all, the universe will send us situations in our lives so we can learn what we need in order to achieve our desires. For example, when I was looking for a girlfriend, I had to go through some experiences before I could find the girl I married. This is something I will speak about later. For now, I would like to go back to negativity and how I got over it. I was speaking to a friend of mine once, and what we were speaking about hit a nerve about negativity. It just hit me that I was too negative. So I decided to do something about it. I recalled a sermon I'd heard by Monsignor Tom Hartman, a famous priest on Long Island who had a show called *The God Squad*. He was speaking about Lent and the different things we give up. He said that, when we give up something, it should be something that is bad for us. For instance, if we smoke, drink, or eat too much, we should consider giving up tobacco, alcohol, or excessive eating and taking control over these habits. This also goes for any harmful behavioral habits, traits, or emotions. I decided to give up negativity for Lent one year, and it really helped. During the season of Lent, every time I started to react negatively to a situation, I reminded myself that I had given negativity up for Lent. My focus was on giving up negativity, and my awareness expanded on that focus. With God's help, because I had faith, I was able to overcome it. This helped me continue on my journey of enlightenment and an understanding of how the universe works.

Anyone can give up bad habits if they really want to but faith can help accelerate the process. This can be done with any faith that has the same principal. I feel that giving up something that's bad for us makes more sense than giving up something we enjoy that's not bad for us, like chocolate. If it's not bad for us, then why give it up? If it's not detrimental to us, then it's not something we should do without. Giving up something that is bad for us will allow us to reap the benefits once the bad thing or habit is eliminated from our lives. This can work for anything, even addictions like smoking, drinking, or drugs. And it can work for harmful traits or emotions like I had.

I did this not only for negativity but also for anger, doubt, and being judgmental. Year after year, during Lent and anytime I experienced any of these emotions, I believe God reminded me that I gave that up, and it should be eliminated from my life. I am so much better off without these emotional traits, which were taught to me in my formative years. Anything that will make us a better person will make us happier. We must send love and good thoughts out to the universe, and we will receive the same.

At one point in my life, I gave up smoking, which was the hardest thing I have ever done. This was when I was much younger, thankfully, and my body was able to recover and clear out my lungs. I quit this terrible habit and started jogging. At first, all I could do was one lap around the track. I have to mention that, after running, the last thing I wanted was a cigarette. I will speak more about this in the health section later on.

Returning to relationships, in order for us to have good, meaningful relationships, we must have a *good, meaningful* relationship with ourselves. We must love ourselves the most, and it's not conceit I am talking about. We cannot love anyone else more than we love ourselves. Our job is to focus on being who we are, being comfortable with ourselves, sending love to ourselves and others, and living our lives on purpose. We must lose all negative traits and emotions and drop all that baggage we carry around with us. And we have to avoid judging others. Everyone just wants to be happy, and sometimes people make mistakes, saying or doing the wrong things. I know from experience that I have done or said things that hurt other people without even realizing it. Now I try to give people the benefit of the doubt, forgive, send love, and move on with life. I believe most people are good deep down; there is a lot of good in the world. We just have to look for it, and we will see it. I was watching the news one night, and they were talking about how rude New Yorkers are. One person said it best, "It's not New Yorkers who are rude. It's crowds that are rude." I believe this is a true statement.

Having a meaningful relationship with myself was something I had to figure out on my own. At one point in my life, I hated myself. I was very unhappy, and of course I did not love myself. My life, day after day, was one that lacked joy and happiness. Even though I was looking for happiness, I couldn't find it, because I had to realize that it came from within, not from outside. I had become so unhappy because of the ignorance, negativity, judgment, and hostility of my upbringing. I knew this was not the way to be, and this sent me on my now never-ending journey of becoming more than I am. Byrne talks about this in *The Secret*. When you get to the place in your life where you know your current path is not your only option and you can change it the way you want, you will know you deserve to be happy. What this meant to me was that everything that had happened brought me to this moment in my life where I realized something was wrong. I was in my twenties when this occurred, and I knew I had to do something. My life had been on autopilot until then. I simply reacted negatively to every situation that came my way like my parents, which was just wrong.

I felt very depressed and unmotivated, but I was trying anything I could to find myself. I went to self-help workshops, frequented the gym, started therapy sessions, and tried anything else I could think of. I felt very agitated; when I was home, it felt like the walls were closing in on me. I always felt I was missing out on something. And that something was life—living my life the way it should be lived. Still, I felt unmotivated. I was speaking to one of my friends about this. She made a good point. Why, she asked, if I was so unmotivated, was I was doing all these things? She asked me what was motivating me to make the efforts I was making. My answer was simple—I wanted to feel good and be happy. That is what everyone wants deep down.

At that point, all my friends had girlfriends, were engaged, or were married with children. I felt like life was passing me by. I had no one I could share my life with. Ever since I was old enough to date, I had wanted a girlfriend—someone to be with, someone whose company I enjoyed and who enjoyed mine. Unfortunately for me, enjoyable dates were few and far between. Most likely this was because of the negativity and judgment I'd picked up from my parents. I caught myself saying things to people that were very offensive without realizing what I was doing—another habit I'd picked up.

One time, I was in a club. I was talking to a pretty girl at the bar, and we were discussing our careers. It was her birthday, and she had a room at the hotel where the club was. We were having a very pleasant conversation. She was working in retail sales, and I was going to start a new job in professional sales selling computer systems. Then I said something very stupid, without realizing what I was saying. I told her something to the effect that I couldn't work in retail sales because I felt it was somewhat beneath me. After that, she stopped talking to me and started talking to another guy at the bar. I heard him say there were a lot of jerks in here, meaning me. What an idiot I was. I guess I was so wrapped up with my new career, which I was very excited about, I didn't realize what I was saying and how it affected the person I was speaking with. This was what mother used to do; she was so wrapped up with her own problems and negativity she didn't know she was hurting other people's feelings with what she was telling them. This is something I had witnessed many times growing up.

If I could go back in time, I would have said something different. Perhaps I would explain that I couldn't be in retail sales because I would have to deal with the general public, which would be very challenging for me, and I would not have the patience. I would also say to her, "I give you a lot of credit for having the patience and perseverance to be working in such an environment." Now, with all that I have learned, I would mean it. Everyone's job can be difficult, and we should be cognizant of this. It doesn't matter what it is, and we should be thankful there are people who have jobs we do not wish to have. I am thankful for everyone's job because it makes our lives much easier. What if no one was in retail sales? Then where would we go to buy things? What if there were no garbage collectors, no bus drivers, or no doctors or nurses? Garbage would pile up, everyone would have to have his or her own transportation, and we wouldn't have our health. I know that, if no one ever discovered antibiotics, I would not be here.

It's important to realize that whatever job people have, we should be thankful of it because it gives service to others. It took me a long time to realize this unfortunately. Many of us are brought up with the notion that we must be successful and that people who don't fit our definition of successful are not worthy. When we are very young, society tells us we are what we do, we are what we have, and we are what we look like. These are false truths. In reality, we are who we are. According to Dr. Wayne Dyer, we come into this world with nothing, and we leave with nothing. It's not what we achieve or what we accumulate that matters but how we treat other people and ourselves. I believe we are here to make this world a better place by utilizing our God-given talents. The truth is, everyone is important and has something to contribute to the world—no matter what that contribution might be. We shouldn't judge people by the work they do, as long as they are happy doing the work. When someone is in a job or career that doesn't make him or her happy, then it is that person's responsibility to find what works for him or her. People need to look deep inside themselves and find what they love and are good at. This will bring them fulfillment. I will speak more about this in the career section.

We should never judge anyone by what he or she does for a living or wears or looks like. Everyone can reach their potential by fully being whoever they are. If we judge others, then we are limiting ourselves to many possibilities. We don't know someone until we spend time with and speak with him or her. So by being a negative, judgmental, and sometimes angry person and by believing that people were against me, I was limiting myself to many possibilities, possibilities that may have benefited both me and those I saw as enemies.

In one of his books, Deepak Chopra says the letter *O* is for opportunities for everyone we meet, because everyone brings new possibilities into our lives. I believe it is very important to be kind to people, to not look down on anyone, and to treat everyone with the love and respect they deserve. We all came from the same source—be that God or energy or whatever you believe. Don't label people; we don't know what is going on in their lives. Sometimes we see people and they seem stuck up or as if they don't like anyone and stick to themselves. We are not mind readers, so we have no idea what is going on in their heads. Sometimes people are just shy or insecure about themselves, which will prevent them from appearing friendly. Someone may be looking at us and thinking, *Why would anyone want to speak to me? I am not worthy,* or *I am ugly,* or *I am too fat.* And we may look at that person and see someone who is successful or someone who has it all together or someone who is beautiful.

I have gotten to know some women who have confided in me that they believe themselves to be ugly or too fat. These were women who I, and many others, saw as very beautiful people. They were perceived as being aloof or stuck up. But in truth, they felt bad about themselves and how they thought the world was seeing them. They were the one's having a tough time with who they were, and they were reflecting that frequency out into the world. I personally used to have a tough time speaking to beautiful girls, as being around them made me feel intimidated, especially before I got married. It isn't how beautiful someone is or how he or she looks that's important but what we say and feel. I would always get nervous speaking to these women because I was so concerned about how they would look at me. Of course, being nervous, I would say something stupid or inappropriate. One time I saw my friend Monsieur Tom Hartman, a priest I was friendly with and the man who married my wife and I, speaking to a gorgeous girl. I mentioned to him how beautiful she was and how I wouldn't be able to speak to her because I would have gotten too nervous. "She is just another person," he told me, "a child of God with a personality and feelings just like everyone else." He advised me to see people for who they were, not what they looked like. This goes for everyone else—men and women; we should see everyone we interact with for who they are, their true selves. And it's very important to be yourself, not someone you're not.

I have to admit, I was also in the position where I may have intimidated people or led them to believe I was stuck up because of how I felt about myself. As I've mentioned, I did not think very highly of myself. Luckily, now I know better. Whatever we are feeling, we are sending out that vibration, or those vibes, to the world, and that is how others see us.

CHAPTER 6

HOW I MET MY WIFE (LIFE PARTNER)

One of the most important relationships we will ever have in our lives is with our spouses or life partners. I believe choosing a partner is the most important decision we can make as far as relationships go. Our parents, relatives, or children are ours, and we have no choice in the matter. As the saying goes, "Friends are God's way of apologizing for our family." It just makes sense that we should be very diligent in looking for someone to spend the rest of our lives with. This is our life partner, someone we will always be with, even longer than we will be with our children. Children grow up and usually move out, get married, and start their own lives. Even though we will be a part of their lives, they still have their own lives.

At a young age, when we are teenagers and are looking for someone to be with, a boyfriend or girlfriend, we look at people and say things like, "He's hot," or, "She's hot," or "I would love to date that person." Physical attraction will always be the first thing that draws us to someone. That's all fine and good, but physical attraction is only the introduction. The real test is when we get to know someone. Everyone is different, which is something we need to keep in mind. If we do finally get to go on a date with that hot person we have been dreaming about, most of the time it won't meet our expectations. Either you expected too much or you and that hot guy or gal were just not compatible. Perhaps you didn't like the same things or had different opinions or views. Maybe the conversation wasn't stimulating. Many times, we realize during a date that the person we're out with is a jerk, obnoxious, not interesting, and on and on. Whatever it is that turns us off, we have to remember that everyone is different and has different views. However, there are times when a date goes well and you and the person you're out with hit it off. This happens occasionally, but it does happen.

They say beauty is in the eye of the beholder, and I have to say that, from my own experience, I believe this to be true. When I was younger, I was attracted to a girl at work who I thought was hot. I would see her every day. I finally started talking to her, and the more I got to know her, the less attractive she was to me. Once we get to know someone, we start to see the person for what he or she is, and how we see that person starts to change. It's not that people are more attractive or less attractive; it's our emotional energy behind how we see people that changes. The more we like or love someone, the better they look to us.

This can also work in reverse. For instance, if we see someone we are not attracted to and we get to know that person and develop a strong emotional connection with him or her, how we see the person starts to change. We become more attracted to the person and start to see him or her as beautiful or more attractive. I'm not saying we fall in love with the person, which is also possible. But we do see him or her differently; maybe the person becomes a close friend or just someone we can talk to. This has happened to me many times in my life, and I am sure it has happened in other people's lives also. Just like in the quantum world, as we look at things differently, those things start to change. I guess it works for people as well. To sum it up, as we get to know someone, his or her appearance to us changes.

Most times, when we have a first date and it doesn't go as we expected, we get disappointed and feel terrible. It's not that the date didn't go as we expected that has us so upset; it's the expectation we had for the date and the fact that we are still not in a relationship. This is especially true as we get older and we find ourselves alone. For most people who are older and without a partner, even though they are disappointed, they still have their family, and that helps a little. For me, I could not stand to be home with my family. I couldn't talk to them about anything; they didn't understand me, or the world, for that matter. Luckily, I did have some friends (God's apology for my family). I too would fall into depression at times because I was not in a relationship. Certain events, such as my cousins' children's christenings, served to remind me that I didn't have anyone in my life. I would go into some kind of funk, sort of a depression, which reminded me even more that I was alone. It would take me days to recover.

I saw all my friends and cousins get married and have children, and I was still alone. This was very depressing for me. Some people give up or settle, but I don't believe we have to go down that path. I truly believe there is someone for everyone. I always looked to God to help me find someone, and one day a friend of mine gave me a paper titled, "On His Plan for Your

Mate." Several versions of the paper, whose author is unknown, exist, but the following is one I found online:

> Everyone longs to give themselves completely to someone, to have a deep soul relationship with another, to be loved thoroughly and exclusively.
>
> But God says, "No, not until you are satisfied and fulfilled and content with living, loved by me alone, with giving yourself totally and unreservedly to me alone.
>
> "I love you, my child, and until you discover that only in me is your satisfaction to be found, you will not be capable of the perfect human relationship that I have planned for you.
>
> "You will never be united with another until you are united with me, exclusive of anyone or anything else, exclusive of any other desires or longings.
>
> "I want you to stop planning, stop wishing, and allow me to give you that most thrilling plan existing, one that you can't imagine. I want you to have the *best*! Please allow me to bring it to you.
>
> "You just keep watching me, expecting that satisfaction, expecting the greatest things, and know that I Am. Keep learning and listening to the things I tell you. You must wait!
>
> "Don't be anxious. Don't worry.
>
> "Don't look around at the things others have received. Don't look at the things you think you

want. You just keep looking off and away up to *me*, or you'll miss what I want to show you.

"And then, when you're ready, I'll surprise you with a love far more wonderful than you would ever imagine.

"You see, until you are ready and until the one I have for you is ready (I am working this very minute to have *both* of you ready at the same time), until you are both satisfied exclusively with me and the life I have planned and prepared for you, you won't be able to experience the love that exemplifies your relationship with me ... and this is perfect love.

"Dear one, I want you to have this most wonderful love. I want you to see in the flesh a picture of your relationship with me and to enjoy materially and concretely the everlasting union of beauty and perfection and love that I offer you with myself. Know that I love you utterly, I am God Almighty. Believe and be satisfied."

I read this many times and kept a copy of it with me. What I didn't realize at the time was that I still had a lot to learn. It wasn't until I had gone through life's lessons, was content, and had a loving relationship with myself and with God that I was ready to meet my mate. Plus, I had to keep the faith. I believe faith is the most important ingredient. No matter what happens, we must have faith. And yes, I did light candles and pray that I would meet someone for me, and it does work. Life is a learning process. In many cases, we need the experience of dating different people, and sometimes difficult relationships and getting hurt before we can move forward. For me, I needed to go through such experiences so that I could grow. Through them, I would come to the place where I needed to be in order to be ready to meet the one for me.

How did I meet my wife? I did a lot of soul-searching and kept myself the best I could be in all areas. I dated quite a few girls and had several relationships, all which were preparing me for life. Thinking back, I should have been less judgmental, more patient, less critical, more open-minded, and a little kinder. I feel I should have treated each of my dates like a job interview, just to see if the date and I were compatible. I could have left the anticipation and emotional charge out of it, so that I could simply accept the person for who she was with loving energy. And if we were not compatible, then we could have left it at that and parted acquaintances. I would have wished her well, knowing she was looking for the same thing I was, a loving relationship. You never know where this might lead. There is a possibility you might become friends with someone you'd thought of dating, and you might meet your soul mate through that person. After all, we do live in a world of all possibilities. There is no shame in going on a date and two people not hitting it off. Everyone is different, and everyone has to find his or her own way. Meeting different people will help us achieve that goal. Treat dating like life's lessons for us and keep an open mind. Every person we meet is a new experience, and there is something we can learn about everyone through our experience of him or her and possibly about ourselves.

Everyone wants to be happy, and being with someone you are compatible with will bring more happiness into your life.

I say more happiness because we must be happy and love ourselves first before we can be happy and love someone else. For instance, if we love ourselves 50 percent, then we can only love someone else 50 percent. Just imagine, once you get married and have children, you have to spread your love to your spouse or significant other and your children. That's a lot of love to distribute, so loving yourself as much as you can is very important; loving yourself 100 percent would be ideal.

When I was looking for a girlfriend, I did many different things to try to meet someone. I went to a coed gym, joined a dating service, attended as many single events as I could, and went out frequently to dance clubs, which is one of the worst places to meet someone. I went to dance clubs because I loved to dance, and I still do. But I was also going in the hope of meeting someone. Going out to try to meet someone at these types of venues usually doesn't work out well because people aren't themselves. Yourself is one of the most important things to be when you are trying to meet someone. You have to be you because, if you are not true to yourself, then you are not being true to the other person. What if the person falls in love with your false self? How long do you think your relationship with that person will last? And if it did last, you would be miserable because you would now be with someone you are really not compatible with. You would be in a situation where you had nothing in common with your partner, and the other person would wind up getting hurt because they fell in love with your false self, which, in reality, was a lie. Getting hurt like this feels horrible, and it also feels terrible to hurt someone.

A couple of times, I had to break up with a girl because the relationship wasn't for me, and I felt horrible doing it. Then I was alone again, which wasn't great. But being alone is better than being miserable. And of course there were times I was on the other end, when I got hurt in a relationship. There was one that really got to me. I was miserable, couldn't focus, felt really bad about myself, and hated myself. And at times, I wanted to end it all—yes, I wanted to commit suicide. There were several times in my life when I wanted to end my life, and I will discuss that further in the health section.

Luckily for me, I was able to overcome all this through a lot of soul-searching, self-help, some therapy, friends, and God. I was able to have some sort of normalcy in my life.

Once I was able to get it all together, I was back on the dating trail. The dating service was a dead end for me, and someone mentioned putting a personal ad in the newspaper, which I did. My first ad was okay. It basically said what I was looking for in a girl. I met a few nice young ladies, but none of these potential relationships panned out.

After some time, I did some more soul-searching and reevaluated myself. I placed a second ad. I gave a brief physical description of myself, listed the most important things to me— what I liked to do the most and some of my attributes I thought were relevant—and stated I was looking for someone with similar interests. I did not state in the ad the kind of woman I was looking for as far as any physical description or likes or dislikes she may have. The idea was for me to keep an open mind and have the reader decide whether or not she was interested in meeting me.

I received about a dozen responses and went on several dates. And one of those dates was with my future wife. I believe I only met with three of the twelve, because after I met my wife,

I stopped looking. We hit it off right away. Our first date was at a bar and restaurant, where we met for drinks. We danced a little and had a very nice time. We continued to see each other, and while we were dating exclusively, it felt different than it had with any other girl I had gone out with. Sometimes when we are in a relationship we get infatuated with the other person or fall madly in love, and then it wears off. Most relationships start out this way. Then they either fizzle out, or if it is right, they stand the test of time. It's very important to have feelings of love between two people evolve into a solid bond that will last. And of course, *we must love ourselves.* As I've stated before, this is very important. We can only love someone as much as we love ourselves, and this goes for not only our relationship with our spouse or significant other but also for all relationships with our family members and friends.

When I was going out with my wife, we were enjoying ourselves and having a lot of fun, which all loving couples should be doing. There also was something else. I had a feeling I'd never had before. I couldn't explain it, other than to say I had a feeling that we belonged together. This was something beyond a feeling of like or love or infatuation. I was relaxed, confident, and content, and our connection was strong. During the time my wife and I spent together both before and after we got married, many people have commented on how we complement each other. If others could see it then it was very apparent. I believe that, if anyone is in a relationship and questioning it, he or she should ask friends and loved ones what they think. How other people see us is the truth. Our friends and loved ones can see us in a relationship objectively, without all the emotional charge. Whether it's infatuation or being head over heels, we can't always see things as they are.

Our significant other should always treat us with love and respect and should never put us down. This is mentioned in *The Secret*, which talks about how we want others to treat us. We should always be with someone who treats us with love and respect, and it is very important that we treat ourselves and others the same way. This is how we must feel about ourselves. If we don't have love and respect for ourselves, then how can others have love and respect for us? We project out into the universe how we feel, and others can sense it. I remember times when I felt great about myself, truly filled with self-love, and people would be attracted to me. They would be very attentive, and I would receive warm greetings. There were also times when I didn't feel good about myself, and there seemed to be no one around. I could tell people were not attracted to me at all; it was more like I was repelling them. It is very important that we feel good because how we feel at any moment is what we are putting out into the universe. And that is what comes back to us. We attract that which we are.

My wife and I have been married for over twenty-three years, and we have a very good, loving relationship. We know each other well. It has been an interesting journey. When two people get married and have a family, things become very challenging. Juggling a spouse, kids, career, and house, not to mention the need to maintain your own identity can be difficult. All these things can weigh us down, and we can start to feel overwhelmed with life. This will make us feel sad or sometimes depressed. We can start to lose the love for ourselves and others and begin mistreating ourselves and others, and sometimes we don't even realize it. As our love diminishes for us, then we have that much less to give everyone else, especially to our families, spouse, and children. We can only give as much love as we have. And if our self-love starts to diminish, we start giving less love to everyone, including ourselves. No matter how tough things get, we must find a way to bring that love back to us.

Being grateful for what we have can be a good way to start bringing that love back to us and to make ourselves feel good. Byrne's *The Magic* can be very helpful. While reading this book, I became more aware of the many things to be thankful for—such as the air we breathe and the water we drink, wash with, and bathe and swim in. These two very important elements give us life, and without them, we could not survive. There are so many other things to be thankful for, like our police officers, firefighters, sanitation workers, and many other public servants. Just think what our life would be like without them. We'd have no protection from crime, fires would burn out of control, and garbage would build up. We can also be thankful for our families. For most of us who have good relationships with and are close to our families, being a member of a family is fantastic. But not all of us have that. I know I didn't. Remember that our friends are God's apology for our families. That's why we should be thankful for our friends. *The Magic* opens our minds to all the wonderful things to be thankful for. We should even be grateful for the people who serve us in restaurants or coffee shops. Where would we be without coffee? For me, no coffee would be tragic. I once heard someone say we should tell people thank you for coming to work today. Just imagine if someone thanked you for coming to work today and for helping out. How would that make you feel? I know it would make me feel good. I also say thank you to people for their time and help after someone assists me. Thanks show that you value and are appreciative of others' abilities. It can only help them feel good and want to help you. I've done this several times, and I usually receive good results. All this starts to bring us to a better place and starts our thinking process going in a more positive direction.

The other very important thing is having a relationship with ourselves. We must discover who we are. We must know what are our talents and desires are and develop them in order to fulfill our purpose and destiny. Once we know who we are and what we want, then everything starts to fall into place. We must keep in mind life is not a destination but a journey. We must consistently evolve and learn, so we can reach our full potential and fulfill our desires. This is something we should keep in mind while we grow with our families, especially with our spouse and children. We need to grow with them and set a good example for all. Children learn mostly by example, just like the study of memetics teaches us. We become a product of our environment, so it is very important we do our due diligence to be the best version of ourselves.

CHAPTER 7

MORE NEGATIVE EMOTIONS TO DEAL WITH

Another terrible trait I grew up with was prejudice. My parents were very prejudice, and so was I because that was what I was taught. Small children don't know any better. They are like sponges, and they absorb whatever is thrown their way. Once I realized how bad prejudice is, I wanted to stop its spread. My wife and I never taught prejudice in our home to our children, so they won't, in turn, spread it to others. I believe everyone is equal. I am no better than anyone else, and no one is better than me. We are all the same. We all come from the same source and share the same source energy throughout the universe. This is what religion and quantum physics teaches us.

I was taught to believe people different from us were bad or not as good as we were. If we treat people in this manner, then they will behave in the way we treat them and fulfill our expectations. This goes back to what kind of universe we decide to believe we live in, hostile or friendly. However we perceive people or situations, they will behave accordingly. If we feel someone or a group of people is inferior to us or wants to take advantage of us, then that person or group will somehow respond in such a way that will bring those beliefs to fruition. Then we wonder why these groups or individuals behave in the way they do. Having expectations that a group of people or an individual is friendly and wants to help us can have the opposite effect; that group or person will behave in a friendly and helpful way. Consider how, when we go to a restaurant or go on vacation, our expectations are that the individuals we encounter will be friendly and helpful, and that is usually the result. We experience positive encounters when we are on vacation because we are in good spirits and looking forward to the experience. Our good thoughts, feelings, expectations, and excitement put us on a high positive frequency, which gives us positive results. This is how we should always feel. But when we encounter negative situations or events, we get down on ourselves. We always have to remember—and this is something I do forget from time to time—that those challenging situations are sending us lessons so that we will grow. We need to be thankful for all the good in our lives.

To be prejudicial is to have a preconceived judgment about a subject, group, or individual. In other words, we judge one another, which is something I used to do. We shouldn't judge anyone. As I have gotten to know different types of people from all parts of the world, backgrounds, and religions, I have found that we are not all that different. We all come from the same Source. Whatever you call it, it's the same loving energy field. Everyone just wants to be accepted and loved for who they are, period.

I would like to encourage everyone not to be a victim of prejudice. If we feel a group or individual doesn't like or accept us for our background, color, political views, or whatever it may be, then we will project that frequency out into the universe, and that is what we will attract. This is the law of attraction, which is in direct correlation with quantum physics. What we think about we attract. So don't be a victim of prejudice. Don't have a chip on your shoulder. And if you do have a chip, *get it off*! As long as we feel like a victim of prejudice, we are judging the people we believe are judging us, and they will continue to do so because we will be attracting their judgment with our thoughts. Again, the thoughts and feelings we are projecting outward will come back to us. According to *The Secret*, this is the frequency we are generating. If we have bad thoughts and feelings, we are generating a low frequency. And if we have good thoughts and feelings, we are generating a high frequency. Whatever frequency we are generating is the same frequency we are bringing back to us. This is why when we are feeling bad, bad things will happen to us, and when we are feeling good, good things will happen to us.

It is very important that we don't feel like a victim of prejudice, because if we do, we will attract prejudice to us. I used to feel like a victim of prejudice. I believed people didn't like me because of my background or how I thought or my views. In reality, I was allowing people to treat me poorly because that was what I was putting out there. And yes, I did have somewhat of a chip on my shoulder. Sometimes I felt like someone owed me something because of my horrible upbringing and the extremely bad acne that plagued me for much of my young life, which I will discuss in the health section. Once I realized I was the one attracting people treating me poorly by feeling like a victim of prejudice, my life was transformed. I never judge, express prejudice, or allow myself to be judged. I always try to keep an open mind about everyone I meet or see; everyone gets to start out with a clean slate, so to speak. The old saying, "You can't judge a book by its cover" is very true.

Another negative trait I would like to briefly discuss is bullying. I don't have much personal experience with bullying. But I when I was young, many children bullied others. We didn't think much about it for the most part, and our parents weren't too concerned with it either. We used to tease each other. Looking back, I believe that not only was I bullied, but I most likely bullied others. I wasn't like a real bully, and I didn't go out of my way to bully others. I think it was a matter of following the crowd. If the group I was in was teasing someone, I just went along with it. We didn't cause physical harm. But name-calling can be more harmful in the long run than physical injury. Things weren't like they are today. There were times when adults had to get involved in order to diffuse the situation. But because of the present social media, bullying has magnified immensely. A lot of harm can be done from anywhere, and it all can be done from a laptop or smartphone.

I did a lot of things I shouldn't have done, and a lot of things were done to me that shouldn't have been. Hindsight is twenty-twenty, and what's done is done. As I've stated, we must learn from our experiences and move forward.

The advice I can give from my limited personal experience with bullying is simple—don't always follow the crowd. If something feels wrong and it's hurting someone, stop it if you can. Or perhaps you might diffuse the situation by making light of it or making a joke. Whatever works will be fine; just be sure your intent is to stop the abuse.

Experts say bullies sometimes feel inferior, but that isn't necessarily true. Bullies can have average or high levels of self-esteem. Some feel powerful when they bully or may just have a lot of anger. Whatever the cause of someone bullying others, their actions are inexcusable. If you're the bully, you should ask yourself how it makes you feel. Does overpowering someone who can't stand up to you, someone who is maybe half your size or has low self-esteem, make you feel good? Perhaps the person you are targeting has had a tough life at home. Or maybe he or she has some sort of medical condition. The other question I must ask if you are a bully is, when you help someone, how does that make you feel? Does it make you feel better than overpowering someone does? If it does, then you will find yourself in a better place, and people will look at you in a new light.

If you are a victim of bullying, the only thing I can say is, "Don't be a victim!" Refuse to be a victim. Try to make light of the situation. Make a joke of what someone may say to you. Don't show whatever is being done to you is upsetting. If someone who is a bully sees he or she is getting to you, then the bully will continue. In the past when someone would bother or tease me, I would show how upset it would make me feel. And the person would continue to do it. I once worked with a bunch of guys who would tease and joke with me about a certain subject that upset me at the time. Meanwhile, I was in therapy and learned how to deal with life situations more effectively. And then the teasing stopped. One day, I was joking with the guys and asked why they didn't tease me anymore. They explained that the teasing no longer upset me, so it was no longer fun. I finally understood that I just needed to be less critical of myself and accept myself as I am. Always be kind and nonjudgmental, and life will flow as it should, with love and understanding.

If you do find yourself in a bad place with a bully, and no matter what you do, it doesn't get better, then please reach out to someone who can help. You owe it to yourself to get the help you need to get past this so you can live your life to its fullest.

Before I end this section on relationships, I would like to point out a few things. I believe our most important relationship is between ourselves and our source—God or whatever loving energy we believe in. This relationship will enable us to have good, loving relationships with others. Never give up hope on anyone or anything. When I was younger, of course, I was very negative and didn't see or understand that we live in a world of all possibilities.

As I grew up and got to the age when I wanted to find a girlfriend, it didn't happen at first. I got very discouraged. I always thought my difficulty was due to my acne. There was a time when my acne was so bad that I had no skin left on my face, just acne and cystic acne. It was awful. I could not look in the mirror or look at anyone in the face, especially a girl. At one point when I was in high school, a girl was talking to me. I of course could not look her in the face, and I wasn't holding up my end of the conversation. She was trying to speak with me and get to know me, and all I could do was give one-word, less-than-enthusiastic answers. Then one of my classmates came by, and I said hello to him with much excitement. The girl who had been speaking with me walked away. At the time, I didn't realize what had happened—what I had done. Later on, I realized what had transpired. And to this day, I still feel terrible about that moment. The girl was trying to get to know me. I don't know why. Maybe she was attracted to me—I could only hope—and I totally blew her off. It wasn't her at all. It was all me. I felt so bad about myself that I couldn't imagine why any girl would find me attractive or interesting. I was very depressed about my condition. I could be friends with guys, but when it came to girls, I was very self-conscious. Of course, now I realize the full impact of this predicament. I most likely hurt her feelings. To this day, I feel horrible about it, and I would apologize immensely if I knew who she was.

When I was in my early twenties and I was dating, I was meeting women who were very sexually experienced, and I was very inexperienced. I felt like everyone but me was having sex. The more women I encountered, the more I found this to be the case. This was happening because of my thoughts; my thoughts put me on a negative, low frequency, and that is what I attracted to me. The more I focused on my shortcomings, the more they would persist. I just wanted to meet someone who was more like me, someone who was not very promiscuous. Eventually I did meet some women who were not very sexually experienced, and finally met and married my wife, which I am very thankful to God for. I did pray for, wish for, and focus on finding my soul mate, and she finally came. I used to get very down on myself. I felt I was missing out on life by not having a girlfriend and not being sexual. Now I realize that having sexual relations with many different people is not what we should be striving for. Usually when we are seeking out lots of different sexual experiences, after we have sex and the relationship ends, we never see or have contact with the people we were having sex with. If we have sex with someone we have to see every day—for example, someone we work with—things between us can become very awkward. There are always exceptions to the rule though.

Having sex or making love to someone should only be done when our feelings for a person get very strong and we get so close to him or her that the only way left to express our love for that person is to make love with him or her. When we get to that point, having sex with the love of our life is wonderful time and time again. It's just the best. What I have learned is that it doesn't matter how many people we sleep with but how many lives we touch in a positive way. Those people will always remember us in a good way. And if we wind up working with or meeting them later in life, they will be happy to see us. They won't run away or hide like most people who we've previously had sex with would do.

The other subject I would like to speak about is having children. I never wanted children, most likely because of my negative upbringing. Throughout my own childhood, I had been exposed to lack, limitations, and little emotional support. Parenting experts and psychologists say the most important thing we should do as parents is nurture high levels of self-esteem in our children. We can do everything else, but if our children don't grow up feeling good about and believing in themselves, we have failed as parents. When I realized this applied to me, it put me on my journey of always learning and growing. Today I have two beautiful girls who I would not trade anything in the world for. They are my whole life, and I will do anything I can for them. I try to provide for them in all the ways my parents could never provide for me. I remembered how I'd felt growing up, that my parents never understood where I was coming from. For instance, my parents never approved of my music and said it was just noise. Of course, as I noted earlier, now it's called classic rock. My children's music is what they like, and I would never tell them they are crazy for listening to it. As a matter of fact, I like a lot of the music my daughters listen to. As for the few things among their preferences that I dislike, I'll tell them I don't care for it. But I make sure they know that, as long as they like it, that's fine. It's about having respect for them and their likes and dislikes. I would never tell my daughters that they're crazy for liking or disliking something. I may advise them not to be too critical on certain subjects and to lighten up, but that's about it. We have to let our children be who they are and express themselves, as long as they're doing so in a way that's positive. For me, it's all about my daughters, and I will always support them in whatever they do.

As parents, our job is to do the best we can to raise good, caring adults, who work on living their life on purpose, or following their dharma. This, in turn, will provide a good service to others, and our children will benefit in many ways, including financially.

When it comes to having children, most of us are scared. We don't know how to be parents or how to provide for kids. I know that I was scared—I didn't know how I was going to do it—and I believe most men have this issue. Men are cowards when it comes to commitment and caring for children, but maybe it's because we want to do a good job and we don't know how we are going to do it. Maybe we're also afraid of giving up our independence and freedom. It was the same for me. But having children and caring for them and seeing them happy because of you adds up to one of the most joyous experiences you can have. You just want to do everything you can for your kids, and you don't need anything in return, because seeing them happy is reward enough.

I remember that just before my wife and I had had our first child, I was resisting having a child because of the reasons I had mentioned. At the time, I was friendly with one of my coworkers who had children, and I saw all he did for them. I told him I didn't want any children because I didn't think I was ready to give up my free time like he did. I admired all he was doing for his children. I told him that when I decided to have children, I would follow his example. In my mind, he was doing everything a father should do. He would even read up on some of his children's subjects from school and help them with what they were studying. Now, after having my own children, I can relate. When they were younger, I would often help them with their homework. I spent many nights and hours helping them, and I don't regret one second of it. It was all worth it!

Verse 17 in the *Tao Te Ching* by Lao Tzu speaks about "Living as an Enlightened Leader." It explains that being a good leader means trusting and having faith in whoever we are leading, even our children. If you have never heard of or read the *Tao*, I highly recommend you do so; it is a good read. After reading an interpretation of the *Tao* by Dr. Wayne Dyer, entitled *Change Your Thoughts—Change Your Life: Living the Wisdom of the Tao*, I have found it very enlightening to say the least. If everyone lived by the way of the *Tao*, we would not need any army or law enforcement to protect us or keep us in line, and the world would live in complete harmony. The text includes 81 verses in all. Verse 17 reads:

With the greatest leader above them,
people barely know one exists.
Next comes one whom they love and praise.
Next comes one whom they fear.
Next comes one whom they despise and defy.

When a leader trusts no one,
no one trusts him.

The great leader speaks little.
He never speaks carelessly.
He works without self-interest
and leaves no trace.
When all is finished, the people say,
"We did it ourselves."

What does this mean? After reading Dr. Dyer's interpretation of this verse, I believe it is saying that being a leader, in whatever capacity we may find ourselves leading, we must lead by example. We must step back and have faith and trust in those we lead. Remember the old adage, "Do as I say not as I do"? This is not a way of leading anyone. As the study of memetics demonstrates, we learn from and become like our environment or whoever is our figure of authority. According to this verse, a great leader should lead by love, encouragement, and inspiration. A great leader should be a quiet observer and allow those he or she leads to make their own decisions and take their own credit for their accomplishments. The leader should never say, "You were successful because of my guidance." The leader should take a backseat and observe and allow others to find their way.

If a leader is one who is loved and praised, then those he or she leads become dependent upon the leader. They can sometimes have difficulty on their own and may struggle to find their own path when the support of the loving leader is no longer there. If someone leads by fear, those he or she leads will be obedient until the leader is no longer there; then all hell will break loose. Studies have shown that if a teacher puts fear in his or her students, the students will be obedient, but once the teacher leaves the classroom, all structure breaks down and turns chaotic. If a leader uses fear tactics, everyone will despise and defy the leader—think dictators. Then, once the leader's reign is over, the leader will be overthrown by those he or she once led—a cycle history has demonstrated. So to be an enlightened leader like the *Tao* suggests, we should lead by example, inspiration, and love. We should encourage those we lead and trust and have faith in their growth. Then we must simply observe and let them fulfill their desires and destiny. You can apply this to your children as well, as soon as they are ready to receive this guidance, which can be anytime, since they become a product of their environment. This is a leadership style I have tried to implement within my own family ever since I learned about it. It's a far cry from what I grew up with. My parents, like most back then, had no idea how to inspire or motivate their children, let alone be enlightened leaders. I believe the most important ingredient in enlightened leadership is your trust and faith in those you lead. As long as you demonstrate the qualities of an enlightened leader, those you lead will acquire the same traits. And above all, you must trust them so they can trust you. Verse 17 says clearly what the opposite will bring: "When a leader trusts no one, no one trusts him."

Someone once told me that God will provide. And some of my research also clarifies this. Dr. Dyer speaks about our Source or God as knowing what we need. If we ask our source for help, especially with caring and providing for others, I believe we will be given all we need. To make this happen, all we have to do is have faith in ourselves, in our loved ones, and in God. We must also remember to be aware of what we ask for and what events are going on in our lives. For me, I asked to be able to care for my family and have a good job with benefits. Of course, this sent me on a journey, during which I went through different jobs and then back to school. When I finally received a position in information technology and I was taking all my classes and studying for my certification, it was not boring at all. As a matter of fact, it was very exciting for me. That's how I knew I was on the right track. This was a field I'd always wanted to be in. Like Byrne says in *The Secret*, if it feels joyous and you can do it all day, then you are in flow with the universe, as if being carried by the current of a fast-moving river. If you have a job or are in a field or position that provides a service, and you can do it all day and then go home and do more, then that's what it feels like to be in line with the universe.

The last thing I'd like to say about relationships might sound simple, but applying this piece of advice will make a profound difference in your relationships with others. When speaking with someone always look into his or her *eyes*. Be as attentive as you can. If you are wearing sunglasses and are out of the sun, please remove them if you can when speaking with someone;

wearing sunglasses is just like not looking into the eyes of the person you're communicating with. When you see someone, always smile at him or her and say hello. Do this with everyone you know, even acquaintances. This shows that you accept the person you greet for who he or she is. And that's all anyone wants—to be accepted by others. Judge no one and exclude no one; we don't know what is going on in others' lives. We may perceive someone as aloof or stuck up, but once we befriend that person, we may find he or she is a good, caring person who has trouble expressing him- or herself. Sometimes the person is just shy and may have some issues. I know this to be true from personal experience. I was very shy, and I had my issues, some of which I mentioned earlier. One of my close friends told me that he discovered from others that I was perceived as a bit aloof myself. It wasn't that I was intentionally being aloof, but I guess the way I dealt with my shyness and insecurities led to me being perceived that way. This was something I was not aware of. But once I knew about it, then I was able to start to change.

I believe almost everyone has good intentions and qualities to offer the world. Sometimes they just may need a little help getting them out. Many people have had difficult lives, and they, unfortunately, carry baggage from their previous experiences. In all my research, I have discovered that we are all individualized expressions of God. We are all connected. So we should help one another bring out our best qualities. We all have something good to offer the world, and with others' help, we can all excel.

In addition, we don't have to be right all the time when we're speaking with someone. Often, if we are having a disagreement or heated discussion, it's better to be kind rather than to be right, according to Dr. Dyer. He says just be kind, send a silent blessing, and send the person on his or her way is usually better. You can say to yourself, *I know we don't see eye to eye, you are being difficult, and I can't get through to you. So why waste the energy?* Just agree to disagree. This will enable you to step away and move on. And who knows? Just maybe, hopefully, the person will change his or her mind. Some people are adamant, and no matter what you say or do, you will not change their mind. This could be true also for our loved ones who we live with. Who knows? The other person may be the one who is right, and we are wrong. I think it's just better to live our lives the way we want and not try to change the world, unless a change will help others. In some cases, there is simply a clear right or wrong choice or answer. For example, two plus two equals four; if someone says the sum is five and a confrontation is about to ensue, then it's better to say yes, two plus two equals five, and move on.

When I was younger I too would fall into the trap of trying to be right. It was very frustrating. I believe this was a direct result of my father's frequent discussions with one of my uncles. My uncle would come over for Sunday dinner, and he and my father would have these heated discussions about who knows what. I was young, so most of the time I had no idea what they were talking about, but I did know most of it was nonsense. It just seemed to be a waste of time. My uncle was a good man. However, he was a little simple. So it would just have been better for my dad to agree with him. And we all could have had a nice day. Wow, what a thought! This was just a part of the dysfunction I grew up with.

Sometimes we know a subject cold, and we like to talk about it. Maybe, for instance, politics is our forte. Sometimes a person who is well versed in a particular subject loves to talk about that topic simply because he or she is usually right during the discussion and likes hearing him- or herself talk. On one of his tapes, Brian Tracy told a story about someone like this. This person always loved to talk about his topic of expertise because he was passionate about it, which is great. But others who knew him would always run away when he started speaking. Even though he knew what he was talking about, everyone was tired of hearing about his particular topic of interest, and of course, he was always right. If you know people like this, just send them a silent blessing and send them on their way, and hopefully someday they will realize why everyone runs away. If you are this person then, hey, just be and let others express themselves. Have a discussion and not a dictation. It's just better to get along and be friendly. If you are very passionate about your topic, then you can always give talks on it. Who knows? Maybe that's your calling. If you love something enough, you may even be able to make a career out it.

Dr. Dyer speaks about being godlike when we have interactions with others. We should always ask ourselves when we behave in a certain way, am I being godlike? This is how we should always be. We are all connected. So doesn't it make sense to treat others how God would treat us. This also applies to ourselves; we should treat ourselves the same way God would treat us—with love and respect. Byrne also speaks about this in *The Secret*. Not only should we have love and respect for others; we must love and respect ourselves as well. If we don't love and respect ourselves, we can't love and respect anyone else. Byrne says we must fill ourselves first before we can give to anyone. We cannot share love, respect, and joy with others if we have none for ourselves. This is so important; I can't stress this point enough. I touched on the importance of self-love earlier; please love and respect yourself. Lacking self-love is like having a shortage of money; you cannot share with others because you don't have enough. But if you have plenty of money, then not only do you have an abundance for yourself, you have more to give others. Not only will you be happy to do so, sharing will make you feel really great.

In *A Course in Miracles*, Dr. Dyer talks about Jesus saying, "If you want to be like me, knowing that we are alike, I will help you. If you want to be different than me, I will wait until you change your mind; and you will change your mind." I believe that is just so powerful and profound. I try to follow Jesus's example knowing he will help me be like Him if I ask. Today in my life, I try to follow all I have learned, to trust in and have faith in God or the Universe, to avoid excluding anyone and never judge anyone, to be nice to people, to be patient and kind and forgive often, and to do only what is right. I try to learn from my mistakes and to accept the bad, asking to learn from it, and to be thankful for all the good in my life. Just imagine what would happen if we all were to live this way; the world be such a better place. I lived all my life in the New York area, which can be very stressful. People tend to be rude and inconsiderate, most likely due to the crowding. One time, I went on a business trip to Salt Lake City, Utah, and the salesman my associates and I were with was nice enough to take us to Temple Square in Salt Lake City. It was one of the most peaceful, joyous, eye-opening experiences I've ever had. We walked around the square. It was just before Christmas, and many teenagers were walking around singing Christmas Carols. And they were really getting into it. Those who weren't singing were saying Merry Christmas to everyone they saw. *Wow, just like New York*, I said to myself facetiously. You don't see this type of behavior in New York, this enthusiasm; it was just wonderful. Everywhere we went, we felt very safe. We didn't have to worry about our wallets, and everyone was polite. It was like another world.

I can only hope that one day, we all, myself included, can behave in the manner I've described in this section 100 percent of the time. This goal is something I work on every day, and I can only hope you will too. I would like to leave this section with a quote by Dr. Wayne Dyer about karma, which I believe sums up most of this discussion on relationships: "How people treat you is their karma; how you react is yours."

PART III

HEALTH

CHAPTER 8

OUR BIOGRAPHY BECOMES OUR BIOLOGY

Dr. Dyer has stated our biography becomes our biology. If you think about it, this is a true statement. If the mind controls the brain and the brain controls the body, then whatever we think about affects the body. Our positive thoughts help the body, bringing us well-being, and our negative thoughts bring us sickness and disease. This goes for all aspects of our health—physical, mental, and spiritual. I've found we must have a good balance in order to be well. Being spiritual is very important. I have come to believe that a good balance of physical, mental and spiritual health is the main ingredient of overall well-being. From what I have read, including my most recent read, *Super Brain* by Deepak Chopra and Rudolph E. Tanzi, we can heal ourselves from many mental and psychological ailments with our minds. Studies have shown that when there is a chemical imbalance in the brain, talking to someone in therapy can have the same effects that drugs have. So our thoughts are truly determining our overall health.

In addition, studies on the placebo effect show that when we truly believe the medication we are taking is the cure, it affects the body—even if it isn't the actual cure. *What the Bleep!? Down the Rabbit Hole* talks about one such experiment. A subject was given a sugar pill but believed it was the cure for his ailment, and the subject's brain produced the chemical that the pill was supposed to produce and distributed it throughout the body. I find this amazing. What it means is that by thinking correctly, we could live healthy, harmonious lives. But most of us are not taught how to do this. According to Dr. Dyer, we were given all we needed during the first nine months of our lives while we were in the womb. We were connected to our Source or God, and we received all we needed physically, spiritually, and mentally. When we are born, we have open minds, and most of us have good health; we are happy, and we are geniuses because we are connected to source. Dr. Dyer goes on to say that after we are born, life gets ahold of us and de-geniuses us. We take on an e.g.o., which Dr. Dyer says stands for "edging God out." The best thing we can do is stay connected. Unfortunately, we are not aware of this, so we move further and further away from God. Dr. Dyer's CDs on inspiration explain that inspiration means being "in-spirit" with our source. I will speak more about this later.

Being connected to my Source was a real eye-opener for me. All my life, I had gone to church. I'd read the Bible and listened to the Gospel and all the sermons. But I didn't really understand it like I do now. I don't go to church as often as I used to, but the knowledge I've gained through all the research I've done, I feel more connected to God than I ever was before. Also, science plays a huge role in this; we are starting to realize that religion and science are very connected. Remember, if God created everything, He also created all the science we learn about. As I mentioned earlier, even the great scientists believe in the connection between science and spirituality. All the research I have done over the past ten years points to how we should be living our lives. I had no idea to live my life from a state of being connected to all things until I read *The Power of Intention* by Dr. Dyer, which started me on this journey. This was just the beginning for me. It led me to *The Secret*, which led me to *What the Bleep?! Down the Rabbit Hole*, which in turn led me to many other books and venues of inspiration and science. How does all this help our physical health? A healthy mind equals a healthy body. In the health section of *The Secret*, Byrne talks about how our body is casting off millions of cells every second, parts of our body is replenished every couple of hours, and in a few years we have a complete new body. So how is it that we attract aging, disease, and degeneration? We do so as a result of how we think. Happy thoughts that are on a high frequency are generating good, healthy cells, and negative, low-frequency thoughts do the opposite. Once I realized this, I no longer saw myself as getting older. I still feel younger than I am, and I have achieved physical accomplishments I never thought I could achieve.

When I was younger, I was never very good at sports. Even though I liked playing them, I just could never be really good. I have come to learn that it was just my belief system holding me back. The belief was that I wasn't any good at sports; I was spastic, so I thought. I really loved baseball, but I just didn't think I could be really good at it. It wasn't that I wanted to play in the majors; I just wanted to be good and have fun. Then I discovered dancing, something that I did sometimes at parties when I was younger. It was okay at the time, but it grew on me. Then I found out dancing was a good way to meet girls, and I really developed a desire for it. Besides its ability to help me meet girls, dancing was very enjoyable for me. Sometimes I would be on the dance floor for hours. When I met my wife, one of the most important things to me at the time was that she liked to dance. We did go out dancing a lot, and I really enjoyed it. Then over the years, once we had children, we didn't go out dancing much, if at all. There was no time or money. As things got better and my children got older, I had more opportunities to go dancing, mostly at parties. What I discovered was amazing. Not only did I renew my love for dancing, I started to get better and better at it. Today I still love to dance, and putting all modesty aside, I am very good at it. I know this because many people tell me so; I even receive compliments from strangers.

I am writing about this because I want to point out that, here I was years ago, thinking I was spastic and not good at sports, which basically involves hand-eye coordination. Now, even though I am not very interested in sports, I still love to dance, which while not really a sport still requires hand-eye coordination. This demonstrates the power of a belief system; what we believe we bring into our lives, just as what we think about expands. My belief was that I was not good at sports, which also used to include dancing, so I carried that with me. And of course that became my reality. Now I know different. What really helped me was my love for dancing, which catapulted me into my new belief system—that I am a good dancer. The point is that our attention to and beliefs about any aspect of our lives will become our reality.

I grew up with many beliefs *that held me back* or *that I later found did not serve me.* For example, when my mother used to tell my sister and I that if it weren't for us she would be walking on money, I internalized this message. As I mentioned earlier, my mother was simply letting out her frustration over not having enough. But as a young child, I believed it meant it was entirely my fault that we didn't have money. How could I be worthy of anything if I was causing such difficulty for my parents? Now, I'm able to step back and observe all this without the emotional charge, something I learned to do in therapy, which I'll explain later. One day my daughter asked me if we could buy her a designer bag, which was very expensive, for her birthday. My parents' response would have been, "What! Are you crazy? Do you think money grows on trees?" I chose not to follow the same pattern as my parents'; instead, I said to my daughter, "If we could afford it, then we would absolutely buy it for you." I did not blame or throw guilt on my children for any lack or misfortune in my life. I was the one responsible for providing for my family. My children were and are good kids. Even though they are teenage girls and act as such, they are responsible and respectful, and they do well in school. They behave so much better than I did when I was their age. They definitely deserve good things, and I try to do my best to provide for them in all ways, including supporting them in their goals and endeavors.

Supporting one's family isn't only about providing monetary items; it's also about trying to instill good values in your children and teaching them about the power of always thinking positive. This helps our health. Remember, positive thoughts or emotions means healthy cells; negative thoughts or emotions means unhealthy cells. When we see people who are always sick or unhealthy, chances are their thoughts are on negative things, like their sickness or disease, and they've shut themselves out from all the good the universe has to offer. On the other hand, if we see someone who is always healthy and free of disease, chances are his or her thoughts are on positive things, like good health and all the good the universe has to offer. Of course, it's always good to be in a positive state of mind. When I was younger, I was always sick and not very strong, or so I was led to believe by my mother. At a young age, I was always going to doctors, and my mother would say how I was always sick. At one point, my mother told me I was very sick as an infant, and that if it hadn't been for one of my uncles, I would have died. Of course, I'm not sure of the facts, since this revelation came from my mother, who usually got the facts mixed up. She did love me very much. But even though she was a good person deep down, she was very confused, ignorant; and negative; she simply didn't know any other way to be.

I grew up with the belief that I was always sick, and of course that was the world I created for myself. Year after year, while I was in school, I would get at least one serious illness—mumps, bronchitis, sinus infections, croup cough, and on and on— every year. Then came the acne, which was my worst affliction ever. It started when I was thirteen. By the time I was fifteen, I was seeing a dermatologist, Dr. Mandel, and he had given me antibiotics. I believe he was helping me, but my parents thought it was a waste of time. My father was the only one who drove, and Wednesdays were the only time I could go to the dermatologist. My father always came home late from work on Wednesdays. He would eat dinner and then say it was too late to go to the doctor. I missed many visits, and my acne got worst. Since my parents didn't think Dr. Mandel was any good, imagine my surprise when, nine years later when I was twenty-four, I went back to him and discovered that he had been written up in medical journals for being one of the top in his field. Once again, my parents had made a bad decision, and I had paid the price.

To continue the story about my acne, it just got worse. When I was sixteen, my parents took me to a beauty salon, where they would work on my face with creams and gels so everything would come to the surface. After the treatments started, my acne just got worse and worse—to the point there was no skin left on my face, just acne. It was awful. I didn't want to be seen. I felt like the elephant man. I just wanted to die, and there were many nights I would pray not to wake up the next day.

There I was, a sixteen-year-old teenager who had this condition of extremely bad acne trying to go to school and live the life of a teenager. It made me feel very self-conscious, and of course, I couldn't look people in the eyes. (Recall the girl I all but ignored. Of course, there was nothing wrong with the girl; it was all me and my insecurities.) I used to dread getting up in the morning and looking in the mirror; I used to tell myself, "I hate you," and I wished I were dead. My condition was so bad that no one in school teased me about it. Children can be cruel and make fun of others; they'll call people names if they're overweight or have pimples. But my condition was so bad that no one ever made a comment about it to me during the duration of high school, which is pretty amazing if you think about it. I think it was so bad that everyone felt sorry for me, and ridiculing me would have only made the ridiculer look bad. Once in gym class, one of the gym teachers came up to me and asked me if I was under someone's care. I also remember my grandfather yelling at my mother in Italian about how bad my face was. I don't know what made my parents take me to the salon, but of course, they listened to others and not me. The salon was very expensive and not covered under our health insurance, and the dermatologist was. Given our financial situation, in my mind, and most likely others would agree, it would have been logical to go with the doctor who had gone to school for many years to learn about treating the condition I had.

After my episode at the salon, which made my face and life unbearable, my parents finally took me to another dermatologist. I wanted to go back to Dr. Mandel, but of course, they took me to someone else, who was at least a dermatologist. This new doctor started my treatments, and my face was starting to heal. But the damage had been done. I now had many scars on my face, and I still had an acne issue. Then the acne spread to my back and was very painful, so painful I could not lie down; nor could one pat me on my back. The pain was excruciating. That also left many scars.

When I got older and was in college and working at UPS, I had my own health insurance. I changed doctors. I was now going to someone in the city who suggested dermabrasion to try to elevate the scaring. The technique did help somewhat, but I still had some scarring. This was another source of self-consciousness for me. But life went on. My acne continued to worsen, and soon I had cystic acne, the worst type you can get. A few years later, I was speaking with one of my good friends who also had a skin condition. He told me about Dr. Mandel, who was by this time top in his field. I changed doctors again and started seeing Dr. Mandel. Seeing him again was very refreshing. I had faith he would be able to help me. He put me on Accutane, the closest drug to a cure for acne.

At this point, I had been on antibiotics for nine years, which most likely destroyed my immune system. After two courses of Accutane, I seemed to have been healed for the most part. At twenty-five years of age, I felt like I could finally start to live my life. No more going back and forth to doctors on a weekly basis. No more treating my skin with medicated creams, lotions, or hot soaks—a time-consuming and somewhat expensive process. Thankfully, I had health insurance, which made my treatments manageable. Now I could focus on living my life and not my skin condition. I felt totally liberated; now nothing was holding me back.

I tell this tale to point out that even though my acne was a physical ailment, it affected me emotionally and mentally. Not only was it painful physically, it was demoralizing, and it was all I could focus on. What we focus on expands; so the more I thought about it, the more I kept bringing it into my life. My mother told me my father had very bad acne when he was young, so that *I too was fated to suffer from acne* became my belief. Between what I was experiencing and my belief system, my condition just kept getting worse and worse. What I needed to have asked myself was whether the belief that my father had bad acne and so would I had brought the condition to my life or whether it was just hereditary. Heredity most likely played a partial role, but instead of always thinking about it, I should have focused on something else, like school, friends, or even girls and just been myself. But I didn't know how to do that. My acne made me feel very self-conscious and affected me for a good part of my life. Every time a girl would turn me down, I would believe it was because of my acne. I carried that frequency with me and projected it out into the world, and I received exactly what I sent out—the law of attraction at work.

I had the belief that my face was turning girls off for a long time. But of course, the more I thought about it, the more I attracted it back to myself. This goes back to what I wrote about in the section on relationships. We always attract what we think about. Focusing on what is wrong in our lives has a negative effect on us; it causes poor health and leads to stress, which will not only make us unhealthy but can also bring on depression. Stress produces unhealthy cells and affects our immune system. That is most likely why I would get sick so much.

All the struggles I faced in my life, combined with my mother being on Valium when I was fifteen, really took its toll on me. I grew up feeling unworthy and believing good things didn't happen to me. I believed I couldn't do anything right. And of course, I had low self-esteem. My mother would go on and on about things that were not going right. And whenever she was yelling at anyone, including my father, my sister, or myself, she wouldn't let up. When she would get going, the badgering would continue until you could get away from her or she got tired. It was very demoralizing and repetitive like the memes I had spoken about in part I, the study of memetics. *I tell you about this difficult and painful chapter in my life in order to demonstrate the real effects negativity can have on a person's health.*

CHAPTER 9

BEING HEALTHY

Being exposed to negativity all my life really put me in a bad way. Here I was trying to go through life and be successful like most of my relatives and friends, but instead I was having a great deal of difficulty with relationships, my attempts to find a girlfriend, and my career. Most of my troubles were directly related to my mental health, which affects everything in our lives. For example, my mother was once having a difficult time with a tenant in our house. First, I have to mention my mother was usually unreasonable, and things had to be her way. She would watch everything the people living in our house would do. She even kept track of what time they would come and go. And she would try to tell them what she believed they should be doing. She used to say to me, as if it were simply not okay, "They come and go as they please." I would try to tell her that she couldn't dictate to people who were paying rent how to conduct themselves. Obviously, if a tenant were doing something like having wild parties or doing or selling drugs, she would be within her rights to say something or ask the tenant to leave. But if the renters were just living their lives, I tried to explain, then she should just leave them alone. My mother treated my sister and I the same way, which was very frustrating.

At any rate, during this particular difficulty with the tenant, my mother just kept getting more and more upset. She became so upset that I believe she had some sort of a nervous breakdown. As best as I can recall, she started shaking and passed out on several occasions. We took her to the hospital three times. In addition, she developed a rash. A slew of doctors from different fields addressed her issues, but we never seemed to get an answer as to what caused her symptoms. I believe her stress level was so high and her inability to deal with all that was going on so low that she had some sort of nervous breakdown. This is what stress can do to us. I am sure many people know this, but to see it firsthand was very interesting.

Here's another example from my teenage years of how mental health impacts us physically. We had a finished basement where my friends and I would get together, and my father had built a screen over the entrance to block the leaves from coming in. I complained about having to move this screen every time my friends came over, but I did it. One night when my friends were over, I had moved the screen and rested it against the fence in front of the house. It just so happened it was garbage night, and the trash collectors took it for garbage. This put my parents on a warpath; they thought I had left the screen there on purpose, which simply wasn't true. I had no idea that it was garbage collection night. My parents screamed and yelled at me for days; that's how long the badgering continued. You would think I'd burned the house down on purpose.

After about a week, my friends felt bad for what had happened, and they came over to help me build another screen. It all hit me that day. I at first felt very strange, and then I couldn't do anything but lie down. Next, I started shaking uncontrollably. After several hours, I started feeling better and could talk a little. I don't know what it could have been. Maybe I had a slight nervous breakdown, if that's such a thing.

Stress clearly affects us physically. Unlike my mother's stress, mine was not self-inflected. My mother worried about everything in her life, and to her, everything was a catastrophe. This put a lot of stress on her, and she had to be a very strong person to endure all these things going on in her head. A good friend of mine, who I have known most of my life, observed this. He once stated that my mother was a very strong-willed individual, so strong she could run a corporation. I believe that if she'd had the proper education, she could have done so much more with her life and would have been a happier person. Unfortunately, she did not have the opportunities others had. She had seven brothers and sisters, and being the oldest, she would help out her mother with her younger siblings. I'm sure she was a great help to her mother. And her mother didn't seem to be grateful. Gratitude was a quality I believe no one in my family was exposed to, because I had to learn how to be grateful on my own.

My mother told me that when she was old enough to work, she got a job and gave most of her paycheck to her mother to help pay the bills. She wanted to go to a dance, and since she couldn't afford to buy a dress, she made one. I am sure she was very excited that she'd made her own dress and was going to a dance. However, her mother didn't want her to go to the dance. So my grandmother ripped up her dress. How could a mother do that to her own child? Back then, children weren't doing drugs or roaming the streets or going to wild parties like some are today. My mother was giving her mother most of her paycheck and helping with all the chores and siblings. The only thing that could make any logical sense was that my grandmother needed my mother to help with the bills and the children, and if my mother went to the dance and met someone and got married, my grandmother would no longer receive help from my mother. From the stories my mother has told me, I don't think my grandmother was in a good state of mind. She definitely needed some help, someone to talk to or some medication.

It wasn't just a proclivity for physical illness that my mother pinned on me. My childhood years, my mother would tell me that I was sick, as in sick in the head or mental. She also said many other derogatory things to me, which I would take to heart. I felt awful about myself and was very angry. I know my mother loved me very much in her own way, but she lacked the knowledge that would have allowed her to nurture high self-esteem in my sister or myself. Dr. Dyer speaks about his mother on his inspirational CDs. She was very inspiring to him and helped him achieve all he has achieved. Even though Dr. Dyer grew up in a foster home part of his life, due to his family's lack of finances, his mother did all she could to reunite her family. She worked several jobs to get her boys back home with her, was always cooking and cleaning, never complained, and always had good things to say. Children learn mostly by example. Her steady pleasantness and happiness not only made her boys like being home, but their friends always wanted to go to their inviting house. I listen to how Dr. Dyer describes his life growing up, and I can see why he has become so successful. He had a good foundation. He did not come from money. Nor was someone in an affluent position guiding him. He had his mom. I believe she was so happy, motivated, and inspired because of her boys. Once they were home with her, she was overjoyed. I believe, to her, providing for them was a labor of love, and she did all she could to keep it that way. I wish my mom had been like that. But unfortunately, she wasn't.

After much soul-searching, I have come to realize how awful my mother's life was. She had it very tough, and her mother did not treat her well. I don't blame her for how she treated me, and of course, I forgive her because she did not know what she was doing. Like Jesus said to his Father when he was on the cross, "Father, forgive them, for they know not what they do." This perfect example of forgiveness is what we should all strive to emulate.

If we are hurting or offending someone without realize what we are doing, then hopefully we will eventually become aware of the effect of our behavior and correct it. If someone is hurting or offending us, then we should be cognizant of the very good possibility they are not aware either. I believe most people are good like my mother. If they are not aware of their offenses, then they will continue to behave in an offending manner. More often than not, people aren't behaving in hurtful ways because they are mean or don't care. Rather, they have become self-absorbed, focusing on their problems so completely that they can't see that others are also going through tough times of their own. They think their problems are the worst.

We all have our crosses to bear. Once, I heard a sermon by a priest about the crosses we carry in our lives. He spoke about a man who was complaining to God about the cross he had to bear. God brought the man to a room that housed all the crosses, from the largest to the smallest. God told him to pick a different one for himself. The man looked at all the crosses, and he didn't want to pick any of the larger ones. But he also didn't want to pick the smallest one because it would show he was looking for an easy way out, and he might be considered a coward. So he picked the next one up from the smallest, and God said okay. The man took the cross and then noticed it was the one he already had. This was a very profound story. It reminds us that even though we may be going through tough times, others are facing their own problems, which may be much worse than ours. I always try to remember to be kind and considerate and to give others some latitude; you never know what others are going through.

This brings me to three other stories I want to share. One day, I was at a gas station. I had been having a good day, and I was waiting in line to pay. The cashier behind the counter was having some difficulty with a couple of customers, so I stepped back. Then just as he was finishing up, a girl walked in and cut in front of me. I told her I was next, and she said something like, "Sorry. Too bad," in a condescending voice. At first, I was very upset. Then I thought about it, and I realized she was having a very bad day. I could say something derogatory back, or I could leave the negativity there, walk away, and continue to have a good day, and she would continue to be in her negative frequency. It was my choice; I could let my ego be in control or I could be my true self. I choose my true self. To defuse the situation, I could have said, "I hope you have a good day," or "I hope your day gets better."

A few years later at another gas station, I was with my wife, waiting to fill up. The driver of the car in front of us pulled away, but she only pulled up a couple of feet before getting out of her car to go to the cashier. I had asked her if she could pull up more. "You have plenty of room," she snapped. "There's three feet in front of you." When I told her that wasn't enough room, she pulled her car up a little more and then called me an asshole. I thought about how to respond for a second or two, and my response was, "Have a nice day." I didn't want to start an argument; it just wasn't worth it. My wife wanted to give the woman a few choice words, but I told her what I was thinking.

The woman still hadn't left enough room to pull out around her car, but I proceeded to pump my gas. She then went to purchase a snack at the cashier. As I was pumping my gas, I saw her come back to her car. Another woman stopped and spoke to her. She then gave her a hug. Evidently, she was going through some sort of negative situation. I don't know what she was going through, but she was having a bad day. It had kind of seemed that way, so when I responded, I wanted to keep it positive to avoid any escalation. I was with my wife, having a nice day. I could have played into the woman's negativity and responded rudely. I could have gotten angry and possibly ruined my day. Or I could respond politely, leave the negative emotional charge with her, and continue to have a good day. Like Dr. Dyer says, send people a silent blessing. I believe the woman we encountered that day needed a silent blessing, and I sent her on her way with one. As for my wife and me, we continued on our way without being aggravated and continued having a good day, while this poor woman continued on her negative journey.

Another time I was driving and someone in front of me cut me off and made me miss the light, which annoyed me. Then she pulled up next to me, put down her window, and asked me where the local hospital was. At this point, I felt bad for even having gotten annoyed. This person was going to the hospital, evidently to visit someone, a loved one who was sick, injured, or possibly on his or her deathbed. She was very upset. I saw it in her face. How could I be upset with her? We never know what is going on in people's lives, so let's just give others a break. This practice is very healthy for us too. It allows us to continue being positive and happy, which in turn, enhances our physical health and creates healthy cells throughout our bodies.

I always try to remind myself of this lesson, which I've learned throughout my life: When a confrontation is heating up, we always have a choice. We can respond with a negative or hostile attitude, which in turn can escalate to a point of no return. If the confrontation goes beyond verbal and becomes physical, someone could get physically hurt. Depending on the situation, you might find yourself in court for months and spending a lot of money on lawyers or possibly facing prison time. This can happen, for instance, with road rage or even a domestic dispute. We have to ask ourselves, which is better—giving into our ego and having an ongoing negative outcome or rising above our ego and responding positively. Be polite; send a silent blessing, which the other person may need; and be on your way to better things, perhaps your goals or all the possibilities the universe has to offer us. When something negative happens to me, such as someone cutting me off on the road, I now leave the negative emotional charge (anger) that I am feeling at the incident and don't carry it with me. Now I can focus on where I want to be, which is a better place. It's all up to us. We can have a really bad day or a really good one, and it's our choice.

Before I end this chapter on being healthy, I would like to speak about something I was recently introduced to—the study of epigenetics. Dr. Bruce Lipton has done a lot of research on this fascinating subject. What is epigenetics? Dr. Lipton explains it as, "the study of inherited changes in phenotype (appearance) or gene expression caused by mechanisms other than changes in the underlying DNA sequence." He says further:

> Medicine does miracles, but it's limited to trauma. The AMA protocol is to regard our physical body like a machine, in the same way that an auto mechanic regards a car. When the parts break, you replace them—a transplant, synthetic joints, and so on—and those are medical miracles.
>
> The problem is that while they have an understanding that the mechanism isn't working, they're blaming the vehicle for what went wrong. They believe that the vehicle, in this case our bodies, is controlled by genes.
>
> But guess what? They don't take into consideration that there's actually a driver in that car. The new science, epigenetics, reveals that the vehicles—or the genes—aren't responsible for the breakdown. It's the driver.

In essence, if you don't know how to drive, you're going to mess up the vehicle. In the simplest translation, we can agree that lifestyle is the key to taking care of ourselves. Think well, eat well, and exercise, and your body won't break down and need new parts.

Dr. Lipton refers to the work of Dr. Dean Ornish to extrapolate. "Dr. Ornish has taken conventional cardiovascular patients, provided them with important lifestyle insights (better diet, stress-reduction techniques, and so on), and without drugs, the cardiovascular disease was resolved. Ornish relayed that if he'd gotten the same results with a drug, every doctor would be prescribing it."

Another definition by Britannica is: "Epigenetics is the study of the chemical modification of specific genes or gene-associated proteins of an organism. Epigenetic modifications can define how the information in genes is expressed and used by cells." In other words, as far as I can understand, we can change our DNA. We don't have to say to ourselves, "I'm like this because it is in my DNA I received from my parents." According to epigenetics, this is no longer the case. What determines who and what we are is our environment and how we perceive it, not genes. You can Google "Dr. Bruce Lipton and epigenetics," and you'll find YouTube videos and a lot of documentation on the subject if you want a more scientific explanation. But I'll try to explain it the best I can.

Epi is a Greek prefix that means "from above or over." Epigenetic research points to a protein above our DNA that influences and makes up our cells in our bodies. What influences the protein is our environment. So if we are in a positive, healthy environment, and we are open to receiving all the good the universe has to offer, we are producing healthy proteins, which are producing healthy cells, which are creating a happy, healthy body for our mental, spiritual, and physical health. Yes, I said spiritual. After all, this—spirit—is ultimately where all the good comes from. However, if we are in a negative environment, and we shut ourselves off from all the good the universe has to offer, we start to produce unhealthy proteins, which in turn produce unhealthy cells. The ultimate result is we feel terrible and attract diseases to us. This is what Byrne talks about in *The Secret*, and here is the scientific evidence that supports it.

The other aspect of epigenetics and our mind-body connection is how the subconscious mind affects us. If the mind controls the brain and the brain controls the body—or should I say influences the cells that make up the body—then what is the subconscious mind doing to us? Epigenetic researchers talk about the subconscious and how it is affecting us. Neuroscience has recognized that the subconscious controls 95 percent of our lives. If that is so, then our conscious mind is only in control 5 percent of the time. This may explain why we tend to fall into the same patterns time and time again. Our subconscious minds are directing us according to how we were programmed from a young age. This is how our neural network is formed from the environment we were raised in and the repetition of our figures of authority who influenced us, our parents for most of us. If we think about the subconscious, the neural net, epigenetics and memetics, these topics all coincide with one another, and we can start to see the direct correlation between them. We become a product of our environment, and we become what we think emotionally, physically, and mentally.

If we are programed by our subconscious, and we are doing things we are not aware of, how do we make changes? For some of us who have had good, positive upbringings; who love and are loved; are happy and not hurting anyone; and are living good, fulfilled lives, then most likely, there is nothing to change. The questions you have to ask yourself are, Am I happy and content? Do I have good, fulfilling relationships? Do I feel my life is fulfilled? Or am I unhappy and depressed? Do I fight with people? Am I aggravated or annoyed most of the time? Are my relationships with friends and family not so good?

During the earlier part of my life, I would have had to answer yes to the second set of questions. While I didn't realize it at the time, my subconscious mind was directing me to think and behave just like my mother—my figure of authority growing up—thought and behaved. Once I realized how unhappy I was and saw that everything was always going wrong, I started my journey of enlightenment. If our subconscious is always directing us, how do we reprogram it? In the same way it was programmed in the first place—repetition. This is analogous to driving a car. When we first start driving, we have to think carefully about each step we take while driving. Eventually we have gone through those steps enough times that they become engrained in our subconscious. This is a simply process of repetition—doing the same thing over and over again. If we want to change a pattern we're stuck in, we need to do something different that's positive and start talking to ourselves in a new light. Positive affirmations are a good way to start. We can say, "I am happy; I am successful; I am worthy," or anything that will reinforce a positive attitude. This will start a new pattern and start to build a new neural network in our brain, which will enable us to think differently. The affirmations must be personal, present, and positive. It can't be, "I will be successful someday," or, "There will be successfulness." It must be, *I* (personal) *am* (present) *successful* (positive). "I am" is very powerful. According to *The Secret*'s Dr. Allan Wolf, "I am" is a creation, which I will explain later. This will put us on a new frequency, start us thinking in different patterns, and hopefully, start to change our lives for the better. It happens little by little, until one day we realize we have changed. I myself am not the same person I was years ago.

Another fascinating aspect of epigenetics is that we can change our DNA for future generations. Epigenetic researchers have discovered that as we change, grow, and evolve, the proteins from the environment start to change, and our cells start to change, hopefully for the better. Then our next generation will inherit these changes and take on the new and hopefully improved DNA, which we have modified. This is an oversimplified version of what the field of epigenetics explains, but that's basically the idea. We can change our DNA and pass it on. Wow, that's amazing. We can't change the fingerprint of our DNA, but now we are in control and not subject to our past generations negative traits. We don't have to think we are the way we are because of genetics. I am living proof of this. My wife asks me all the time, "Where did you come from? Because you are nothing like your parents." I knew my life was not what I wanted it to be, so I changed it. I am sharing this because I know others have gone or are going through some of the same crappy experiences I went through. If you don't believe this, then I suggest you do some of your own research on epigenetics. You will be pleasantly surprised.

CHAPTER 10

THERAPY

Our lives can become very challenging and overwhelming at times. If we did not have a good, positive, inspiring upbringing, and if we don't have a good support system, then life can become very difficult. My life was like this. As you know well by now, I did not have a good positive upbringing, and it was very uninspiring. My father usually sided with my mother, most likely to avoid a bigger confrontation. He knew how difficult she could be, and if he had disagreed with her, the situation would most likely have escalated to a point of no return. Unfortunately, my father was very ignorant, wasn't very ambitious, and did not have much education to speak of. Nor did my mother. Any decision making of his was very limited. Throughout my years growing up, I believed I was consistently being challenged and failing at everything. It seemed like that to me because I was only focusing on the failures and not the successes, just like my parents would do. What was very interesting is, in my early years at school, I did very well. Then as I got older, my grades started to fall. I contribute this to all the negativity, feelings of inadequacy, and lack of an educational support system at home. Once I was in the higher grades, my parents had no clue how to help me. In addition, because they hadn't attained an education for themselves, they could not understand how important school was. I was moving through life on autopilot, with absolutely no direction or encouragement. The only thing my parents were concerned about was that I got a steady job, which is important. But it is also very important to do something you like—something that is inspiring, fulfilling, and rewarding and has advancement opportunities. In other words, it's important to be happy in your work.

My grades started to fall because of the belief system I was growing up with. Being exposed to this negativity all my life started to take a toll on me. There was also some rebellion on my part because I realized how wrong my parents were. All this contributed to my belief system, which reinforced the beliefs my parents had implanted—I was not smart, not worthy, could not achieve my goals, and would live life like my parents did. I would live day to day, never having enough and never having any sort of career. I wouldn't have many meaningful relationships. My life would be uninspiring, filled with complaints, and just plain humdrum. Recall that life can de-genius us. I was doing very well until my belief system changed. Who knows what would have happened if I'd had a more inspiring upbringing, and the genius I was born with—just as everyone is born with genius— had been nurtured? The possibilities are endless. Unfortunately, this was not my case.

I became this negative, angry, complaining person. Just like my mother. Going through life like this was awful. I believed all bad things happened to me. I also believed I had missed out on life because of my bad skin. For ten years, I had to deal with acne issues and my beliefs about my condition, and that prevented me from doing many other things my friends could do. I spent countless hours on hot soaks, going to doctors, and keeping my skin as clean as possible. I was instructed by the doctors not to sweat, as it just irritated my condition, and I was always applying creams to my skin. After ten years of this, I was finally over it for the most part. At twenty-five, I could start living my life. And that was exactly what I did.

I started going out more with my friends, joined a gym, went back to school, ate a wider variety of foods, and went on real vacations. Even though I was starting to live my life, I still believed I'd missed out for so many years. Plus, with constant exposure to my parents, I had a lot of resentment, anger, envy, and of course, negativity. I did not have many good relationships with friends or even a girlfriend, for that matter. I was looking for a partner desperately, and that was exactly why I did not have a girlfriend. Negative, resentful, desperate thoughts were my constant companion; what we think and focus on expands, and that is what we bring into our lives. The more I thought about how desperate and lonely and incapable I was the more I brought desperation, loneliness, and inability into my life. What I needed to focus on was having all the things I wanted, and not the lack of them. *The Secret* tells us we should think positively all the time, but during the early periods of my life, I was not aware of this.

I finally came to a place in my life where I was utterly unhappy; I was miserable and completely unmotivated. Yet I found enough motivation to start making changes in my life—to aim for a better life. So I started therapy, something I recommend for anyone who is going through a tough time and feeling unhappy and/or confused. If you think everyone is against you or nothing is working out, then maybe therapy can help. It's always good to speak to someone when we are troubled. I went to therapy for a little over two years, and even though it had its moments, I just knew I had to do this. I believe to this day that therapy helped me tremendously. It started a new belief system for me and gave me a new awareness, which is something I've come to realize after all my research.

Dr. Dyer speaks about our belief system and awareness. Once our belief system starts to change, just like my belief system about my dancing did, then a new awareness starts for us. We become enlightened, a field of all possibilities exists, and we are aware that we can and should change our beliefs from negative to positive. We are aware that our past thoughts and actions have no bearing on our future and what we can achieve. To anyone who was abused physically, sexually, mentally, or spiritually, or who had a negative, derogatory, or angry upbringing, I say this: You can change it with better thoughts and right thinking. *You are not your past!* You can be anything you want. It may not be an easy task, but you owe it to yourself to have a rewarding, happy life.

We must also be aware of the people who treated us poorly and where they were coming from. We must not place blame, and we must offer forgiveness. Chances are either they were not aware of what they were doing or couldn't control it. This was true for my mother. Once I realized what she must have gone through, I felt deeply sorry for her. Not only was she not aware of what she was doing, which resulted in an unrewarding life, but she unfortunately didn't have a mind that was open enough or anyone to guide her to change. Just imagine what sort of demons abusers must be living with. Their torment may be worse than what they are delivering to others. Forgiveness is huge in this case; it will free you so you can move on to be in a better place. Don't get stuck in the past and keep rehashing what was done to you or what you had to go through. I know it's hard to do sometimes, but we owe it to ourselves to get past our pasts. When we place blame, we look to the past and what cannot be undone. But when we take responsibility, we look to the future and what can be changed. Take responsibility for your life and be happy. The big question is, how do we do this? Offer forgiveness often, live your life on purpose, set goals for yourself, get inspired, live a self-actualized life, and fill yourself up with greatness because this is the way life should be.

While I was going through therapy, I really didn't know what to expect. All I knew was that I had to do it. I knew deep down in the fiber of my being that I needed to go through this in order to live a normal life. My therapist gave me an ability to remove myself and observe my life as though I was looking at someone else. When I started doing this, I realized my life wasn't all bad. I had a good job with benefits, a nice car, and a place to live. I had opportunities to go back to school and a mom and dad. My parents gave me a hard time and were very annoying, but they were still my parents, and I lived in their home. Even though I was miserable, little by little, I was making progress in therapy. As my sessions continued, I had a lot of hurdles to overcome. I was dating girls and finally found a steady girlfriend, who later became my wife. I'd lost a job, found a job, and stopped and started therapy. It seemed like I was on a roller coaster. Going through all this, there were times I did not know if therapy was helping.

Then something happened. My sessions got better and better. I had read the Bible form time to time, and I went to church on Sundays. But I didn't really understand it all. And then it all started to sink in. My therapist noted that I'd come quite far in a short time, and she wasn't sure why. At the time, I was also going for spiritual counseling, which contributed to my improved therapy sessions. I now realize I was getting closer to God and having more faith in Him, and that was what helped me with therapy. All the research I have done points to the origin of God, which goes back to the universal loving energy that always was, is, and will be.

I would like to share one last thing before I end this chapter—some thoughts on being healthy and slowing down the aging process. In *Super Brain*, Chopra and Tanzi say that to reduce the risks of aging, we should eat a balanced diet, cutting back on fats, sugar, and processed foods. The preferred diet is Mediterranean, which includes olive oil instead of butter; fish (or soy-based sources of protein) instead of red meat; and whole grains, legumes, mixed nuts, fresh fruits, and whole vegetables to provide plenty of fiber. Avoid overeating and exercise moderately at least one hour three times a week. Don't smoke. As for alcohol, red wine is preferable, in moderation, if at all. Get a good night's sleep. I know sometimes it's difficult to eat like this, but if we give it a very good effort, not only will we feel better, we will live longer and have good health. The bottom line is, if I'm going to live a long time, I want to be healthy.

CHAPTER 11

WEIGHT CONTROL

For many people controlling our weight is a huge, challenging task. And most of us are losing not weight but the battle. For myself, I weigh less now than I did when I was in sixth grade, when I was huge. I had a thirty-eight-inch waist, and I weighed 160 pounds. Now I maintain a thirty-two-inch waist and weigh less than 160. Coming from an Italian background, my mother was always telling me to eat, eat, eat, in both Italian and English. Given this, I could only be fat. The thought process was the more you eat, the bigger (healthier) you are. Today we know better. We are what we eat, and being overweight is not healthy. It's bad for our overall health. I'm not saying everyone who is overweight should lose weight; the weight that feels right for you is the right weight. The question we need to ask ourselves is, are we healthy and do we feel good? This is most important, especially if you have a family. You owe it to yourself and your family to be with them and enjoy them in a healthy state. I know someone who is close to our family who lost her husband before his fiftieth birthday to a heart attack. He left his wife with two children, one in college and one in high school, and many bills. And yes, he was overweight. Don't miss out on being with your family; you owe it to them and yourself to be healthy.

I was always fat in my younger years; my mother even took me to a special doctor so I could lose weight. Nothing anyone did motivated me to lose weight. We can't motivate anyone else to lose weight, no matter how hard we try. People have to want to do it. Once I was interested in girls, I decided to go on a diet. That was my motivation, and it worked really well for me. I counted my calories, weighed my food, and came up with some healthy low-fat drinks. I did this all on my own with almost no help from my parents. I was twelve at the time I started my diet, and by the time I was thirteen, I had lost 40 pounds. I went from 160 pounds to 120 pounds in about six months. I received many compliments, which made me feel great. What an ego boost, which was great for me at the time. Losing weight also made me feel healthier, and I had more energy. Just imagine carrying a 10- or 20-pound bowling ball around with you all day. How would you feel? Pretty tired I'm guessing. I was carrying a 40-pound bowling ball.

Since I was young and my metabolism was high, most of the weight came off quickly. The last 5 pounds was really hard, but I was still growing, and I kept the weight off. Then when I was fifteen, I noticed I could eat anything and not gain any weight. That was true until I turned twenty-five. That's when I had to start watching my weight again. My metabolism was so high at one point that when I was eighteen, I could go to McDonalds for lunch and have a Big Mac, a Quarter Pounder with cheese, a cheeseburger, a hot apple pie, and a vanilla shake and not gain any weight. Wow, I wish I could eat like that again. Maybe in my next life, but those days are gone. When I was in my early twenties, I went to a nutritionist because I was really tired all the time. He put me on a nutritional diet and instructed me to take many vitamins. I was able to eat as much as I wanted, as long as it didn't contain any fat or sugar. Unfortunately, that didn't leave too many choices, but I did it. After a couple of weeks, I felt great, had plenty of energy, and started to lose even more weight. I ate as much as I wanted and kept to my diet. For snacks, I would usually eat fruit. This was great, especially in the summer. After a couple of months, I was down to a twenty-eight-inch waist. I was never that skinny in my adult life. It was a very healthy diet but very difficult to follow, and it was hard to keep it up. Life comes along, and we have other priorities and lose interest. That's just the way it is sometimes.

To this day, I still have to watch what and how much I eat. It has become a way of life, and I have found what works for me. After I got married and had children, going to the gym or doing any sort of exercise went out the window. That's life! I did gain some weight, and so did my wife. I was up to a thirty-four-inch waist. I lived like this for a while. And then as the kids got older, my wife started Weight Watchers, and she cooked for her diet. We all ate the same food, and we all lost weight. She was very successful with it, and I went down to a thirty-two-inch waist, which I've maintained ever since. I try to work out three times a week, and that's very helpful for maintaining both my weight and my overall health. When I started working out, my overall health started to improve, my blood pressure and heart rate were better, and my cholesterol was down to a very good number. All in all, my health was better. You don't have to kill yourself; just do what you can. Working out three times a week is all I can fit into my schedule, but if I could, I would do more. Whatever works for you is good; anything is better than nothing.

To keep myself in check, I weigh myself every day. Weight loss experts say you shouldn't do that, but that works for me. As soon as I am up a couple of pounds, I know I need to keep an eye on what I'm eating. My diet, for the most part, is pretty good, and I do indulge once in a while and eat anything I want. Everything is done in moderation. Dr. Oz says we should eat until we are 80 percent full. Even though this is hard to judge, I do my best when I can. I keep in mind that if I stop too soon, I can always eat more later, but I can't un-eat what I just ate. Usually at dinner, if I know there is dessert, I will eat a little less dinner to save room for a treat. Monitoring the amount you eat sounds like a simple thing to do, but all too often I forget or I am not aware, because we are programmed to finish all our food and to eat until we're full. However, when I do remember to stop eating at 80 percent, I am still hungry for dessert. And after I eat my dessert, I don't feel stuffed. I feel satisfied, and it tasted extra good because I was still hungry. All too often, we eat until we are full, especially in a restaurant. It takes ten to twenty minutes for our stomachs to tell our brains we are full, and by that time, we are stuffed and forcing down dessert.

The Secret references Wallace Wattles, who says in one of his books that when we are eating, we should be totally present in the moment. We should eat and chew our food until it is almost liquid so our bodies can fully absorb the nutrients the food has to offer and aid in proper digestion in a healthy manner. This sounds very simple, but all too often in our busy lives, we are eating on the run or while reading or watching TV or working, to name a few. We rarely sit down and just focus on the food we are consuming. Being fully present when eating will prevent us from overdoing it because we will be conscious of what we are doing. It is also very important to only eat, especially snacks, when we are truly hungry. Many people snack because they are bored, depressed, or stressed. Whatever the case may be, only eat if you are hungry. I know from my own experience that if I have dinner and eat until I'm 80 percent full or less, I am hungry later for dessert or a snack, and I enjoy it more because I still have an appetite. This will also help prevent weight gain, which is the best outcome I can hope for. The end result is I am satisfied and not stuffed.

When we want to lose weight, we should focus on the weight we want to be and not focus on losing weight. Focusing on losing weight will only attract wanting to lose more weight. This will keep us stuck in the cycle of always having to lose weight. If we focus on the weight we want to be, we are saying to the universe, "This is the weight I am." It is also a good idea to say the affirmation to ourselves, "I am 'x' number of pounds." For instance, I would say to myself, "I am 135 pounds." This will put you on that frequency, so your desired weight can be brought to you. Your goal also must be believable. If you have trouble believing in your ability to achieve your desired weight, try working toward increments of five or ten pounds. When we say the words "I am," it is a creation according to Dr. Fred Allen Wolf, who I mentioned earlier. Dr. Wolf is a quantum physicist who is featured in *The Secret*. He goes on to say that you can't have a universe without mind entering into it. So it is very important when we say the words "I am" that whatever follows is what we want to bring into our lives. Often we say things like "I am late," "I am tired," "I am not as smart, strong, or wealthy as

I would like to be." But we need to change that to, "I am always on time," "I am full of energy," and "I am smart, strong, wealthy, or healthy." Changing the way we speak to ourselves will start a new positive thinking pattern. We should always speak to ourselves positively with love and respect, just like we would to someone we love. We attract what we think about and say to ourselves, so please be good to yourself; you deserve it.

All this is wonderful if we can stay with it and be conscious of our thoughts. The most important ingredient for being our perfect health and weight is to love ourselves. Dr. Dyer speaks about this on "The Secrets of an Inspirational (In-Spirit) Life" audio CDs. It's not that we must be our perfect weight, health, or looking our best to love ourselves; we must love ourselves first in order look and feel great. When we love ourselves, we take care of our bodies the best we can. We eat right, exercise, and groom ourselves because we are full of life, energy, and joy. When we are full of love, we radiate love out to the world, and everyone becomes attractive to us because we are radiating love. And we become a joy to be around.

CHAPTER 12

BEING TIRED

Many people complain about being tired, and I myself fall into this category. We should get plenty of rest, but everyone is different. Some can sleep four hours and be awake and full of energy all day, and others can sleep eight to nine hours and still feel tired and unmotivated, with little or no energy. I am describing two extremes. I wish I would fall into the four-hour-a-night category, but unfortunately, I don't. My parents never seemed to need a lot of sleep, but as a child I had my fair share, just like most children. When I started working and going to school, I was sleeping less. Going through the years, I was tired, and I always believed this was because I did too much. After I got married and had children, there was plenty of sleep deprivation due to having small children and getting up in the middle of the night. Anyone who has babies knows exactly what I am talking about. After a while, you feel like a zombie. You may even forget what day it is or even your name—ha, ha.

This type of fatigue is normal, but if you do get enough sleep and are still tired, falling asleep at your desk at work or having to take a nap during the day, that is not normal. This is what was happening to me. I had blood work done, took sleep studies, and went to several doctors, including an allergist. All my tests came back negative, and my doctors did not find anything conclusive. My pulmonologist prescribed Nuvigil, a drug that stimulates the body so you can stay awake. It worked great the first day, and then there wasn't much of an improvement after that, so I stopped taking it.

While I was going through all this, the doctors asked me if I was depressed. My answer was no. I was depressed in my younger days before I got married. I know what it feels like to be depressed, I had talked about depression and ways to counteract it in my therapy. I am starting to think maybe it's more stress than depression, because I have been very motivated in my career and self-development, always learning new things. If I was depressed, then how was I able to continue my journey of enlightenment, meditate, and write a book? An APA (American Psychological Association) survey found that 53 percent of workers reported fatigue due to work stress, which can also lower the immune system. Add work stress to everyday stress and that will only magnify the results, which can then lead to many more ailments. If that doesn't make you tired, I don't know what will.

Over the last twenty years since my children were born, I'd had many struggles. Money was tight, so I went back to school for more training in my field to get a better position. This enabled my wife to stay home with our children. Juggling work, school, and caring for two small children was difficult. As the children got older, my wife went back to work but only part-time. I acquired a position on the zoning board of appeals in my village, ran for school board trustee in our school district, helped my children with their homework, and joined the Dad's

Club when my children were in high school. I was completely focused on my family and making a better life for us. When I was a young child, we were always struggling, which meant to me that life was a struggle. My belief system was the same as my parents' had been, and I brought it into my life. Once I started thinking more positively, my life started getting better and better. Our beliefs will take us to what our thoughts are and create that reality for us. (Recall that the law of attraction dictates that we attract that which we are or think about.) After all I had learned, I knew that I had not signed up for a life of lack but for a life of fulfillment and happiness, one that enabled me to develop my talents and abilities to help others, including my family. Thus, I did not believe depression could be a factor in my fatigue.

In *Super Brain*, Chopra and Tanzi talk about depression, stress and anxiety—traits I am all too familiar with. I have explored this for myself and have found it was all my negative thoughts which produced stress and, in turn, fatigue. Even though I feel motivated, I never took take much time for myself. Since my brain was wired negatively from my youth and I have been rewiring it for many years, certain negative events can set off the old thinking patterns. When life gets hard and overwhelming, the negative network in my brain's subconscious takes over, and I am back to that old negative thinking pattern. We can only have one thought at a time— either positive or negative— so it is very important to keep our thoughts positive. Negative thinking, stress, and anxiety make us tired. It is like putting poison in our heads. I know for myself that when I am doing something I enjoy or something that's inspiring, I am full of life and energy. Recently, I attended a conference with workshops on various subjects, including self-help. Even though it was on a Saturday, I was motivated to go. I did have a hard time getting up, but once I was there and participating in the workshops and speaking with everyone, I was full of energy, motivated, and really enjoyed myself. The point is, when we are in our flow of where God wants us to be with all our positive thoughts, we are not tired but inspired.

One time after I got home from work, I wanted to exercise, but I was very tired. Then I realized that my tiredness was stemming from my negative thinking as a result of the terrible day I'd had. I then remembered it was my thoughts that were making me fatigued. So immediately I changed my thinking pattern, and I felt more awake and was able to exercise. This is something everyone needs to remain conscious of. Our thoughts and subconscious are always controlling our lives.

When we think about the issues in our lives—lack of money, poor health, envy, jealousy, and feelings of being overwhelmed—it will exhaust us. Sometimes I fall into this trap of thinking negativity, and of course it is exhausting. The key is to keep our thoughts positive and always think about where we want to go, not where we don't want to go. Don't be part of the "don't-want generation." When we get up in the morning and our thoughts are negative, not only are we not full of energy—the day will follow suit. However, if we are excited and have positive thoughts, high levels of energy will flow easily throughout the day. In one of Dr. Chopra's books, he suggests that, in the morning, just before we get out of bed, we ask God to guide us for the day. I would go one step further and add that we should only think about the good things we want and not the bad. We need to find what motivates and inspires us and run with it. I will speak more about this in the career section where I address finding your passion.

For me, I will continue to explore my tiredness. My writing excites, inspires, and gives me energy. When I get up in the morning and I'm thinking about writing, I feel more awake than when I wake just thinking about going to work and doing some mundane tasks. Even though I still like my job, I find myself evolving into something more, opening myself up to new possibilities. I see my life changing before my eyes for the better in all areas of my life. If you are always feeling tired, look at your life. Do you like your job? If you are pursuing higher education, do you like your major? Look around see what excites you. Try to focus on that, and it will change your life for the better. You can do anything you want; as long as it doesn't hurt anyone else, you will be fine. Just remember, if you do hurt someone knowingly, karma will come for you; it's the law of the universe, and there's no way around it.

Before I end this chapter, I would like to say that I am very grateful for my overall health. Many people have serious illnesses and are battling health issues every day. Many stories in *The Secret* tell of people having healed themselves from incurable diseases. The main thing they all had in common was they believed and had faith they would be healed. They also included laughter as part of their healing. As they laughed, they produced good, healthy cells and pushed out the disease. They watched very funny movies for months, eliminated all stress from their lives, and focused on well-being and not on the disease. These are the most important ingredients for anything we want to attract into our lives. Prayer also helps. But when we pray, we must not pray to be healed from the disease but to return our bodies to the well-being we once enjoyed. According to Dr. Dyer in "The Secrets of an Inspirational (In-Spirit) Life," when we talk to God, we should think like God thinks. God doesn't know about lack, disease, or negativity. God only knows about well-being, abundance, peace, love, and faith. Saint Francis was always being hounded by people to be healed. He was overwhelmed, and he just wanted some peace in his life. Instead of running away and praying that people would leave him alone, he prayed to God and said, "God, make me an instrument of thy peace, Amen." Hence, we have the "Prayer of Saint Francis," also known as "Make Me an Instrument of Your Peace."

When we pray to God, the universe, or whatever we believe in, always pray not from a position of lack but from a position of abundance. If you want health, pray for well-being; if you want money, pray for abundance; if you are lonely, frustrated, or overwhelmed, pray for love and peace; and if you are tired, pray for high levels of energy and well-being. My wish to all who are struggling is that you can be better than you are, have well-being, develop your talents, and help others. I wish you fulfillment, happiness, and the capacity to contribute your great abilities to the world. God bless!

PART IV

CAREER

CHAPTER 13

THE CAREER FOR YOU

When we are born, we don't come with an instruction book or a manual. We are who we are, and it's up to us to find out what we are all about. From all the psychological, scientific, religious, and spiritual research I have done, I have learned that to be fulfilled and happy, we should just be. What are all the experts talking about? We should be, of course, who we are. It is up to us to discover who we are. But more importantly, we must discover what we signed up for in this life. Ask yourself, What am I here to do? What are my talents, abilities, likes, and dislikes? What makes me happy, loved, and fulfilled? What I am interested in? According to Gautama Buddha, "Your purpose in life is to find your purpose and give your whole heart and soul to it."

Growing up and trying to figure out what we want to do with the rest of our lives can be very confusing and frightening. All these questions will help us find out who and what we are and what we should do with our lives. For me, these were some of the questions I asked myself. I had no guidance from my parents as I was growing up. I had to figure most of this out for myself. Throughout our lives, our careers may change as we grow and evolve. If you see things changing in your life, sometimes you need to just go with it. Maybe it's the universe speaking to us and guiding us in a different direction we need to go. It's okay to change careers or direction; sometimes a change is what we need. And we must know when to trust and have faith in the universe or God to guide us. As long as we are growing and evolving, change will happen. And sometimes change is a good thing, so just go with it. As George Bernard Shaw said, "Progress is impossible without change, and those who cannot change their minds cannot change anything."

Having a fulfilling career will not only bring us satisfaction and money, it will also bring us happiness. And the bottom line is that happiness is all we truly want deep down. Career success will make one part of our lives complete. But we must always remember to have good, fulfilling relationships as well. To be truly successful in our lives, we should be well-rounded and have balance in our lives. Many people go after the money and get rich, but their relationships stink. Then there are some who are very spiritual and have good relationships but are always sick and broke all the time. In *The Secret*, James Ray talks about this, and neither one is successful in my opinion. Having a good balance is very important to our overall well-being.

So how do we go about achieving balance? For me, I always looked to God to guide me to do His work and to find my purpose; it was like being on a mission from God. If you ask God, the universe, or whatever higher calling you believe in to trust and guide you, things will start to change. Be aware of what you ask for because the universe will start to rearrange your life and send you the lessons you need to put you on the path to fulfilling your desires. It is very possible you will be challenged, but that will be the universe sending you the learning experiences you need to move forward.

In the past, I was being challenged and wasn't even aware of it. I went through many difficult times; I lost several jobs (including the one I lost two months before my wedding), had to go back to school after my children were born, and found myself changing jobs again and again until I found a position with a salary and benefits that would allow me to support my family. Even though those times were difficult, I believe God was always there giving me whatever I needed. Dr. Dyer says we will be given all we need from our source. Source knows all we need. It knows that the animals need a fur coat for the winter, the sun needs to shine, the rain needs to nourish the earth, the trees need to give off oxygen, and so on. It gives us all we need, and this doesn't happen by chance; it happens by law. This happens and continues to happen because everything is just as it is, as it should be. We should just be, be ourselves, connect with the universal energy, and open ourselves to the possibilities, and all will be given to us. All we have to do to receive is to have faith in source. Having faith is the most important ingredient for us humans. Everything else, all the animals and plants, don't have to rely on faith because they are just that—as they are. They are just being who and what they are, accepting whatever comes their way. In other words, they are just operating on blind faith (in the order of the universe). And that order just flows for them. That's why it is so important for us to be ourselves—to be how God made us with all His loving energy, to accept what comes our way, to learn from it, to have faith, and to connect with everything around us.

It's like when Jesus sent the apostles out to preach the word of God. He instructed them to take nothing, and all they needed would be provided. And it was. The apostles just went out with faith, trusting and knowing all would be given, with no doubt whatsoever. They trusted and believed in Jesus. And that's the type of faith we need to do God's work. Live our lives on purpose, and all will fall into place. We will be happy and fulfilled. Look for clues, like relationships. Listen to what people are saying to you and what is coming into your life. Sometimes others see things in us we don't see, so we should pay attention to what is happening around us.

Here is a story I found in LinkedIn Influencers, about someone who had an important change in circumstances that at first seemed detrimental but then turned out to be the very beneficial:

> The worst setback in my career took place after I had graduated from medical school in India in the 1970s, came to America, and set my heart on doing research in endocrinology. I destroyed my dream overnight, with very long-term consequences.
>
> The most prestigious research fellowships were those in Boston medicine, and I was fortunate. I was offered one in an endocrinology program at a hospital affiliated with Tufts University that took only two or three new fellows a year. It was headed by a world-famous researcher in the field. My time would be divided between laboratory

work, which would lead to publishing research papers, and seeing patients in the clinic.

I was fascinated by being in the lab, and there was no way to foresee the blowup that would end my fellowship and almost my whole career. What mattered was the subtle interplay of hormones in the body, which is what endocrine research is all about. The field had miles to go before a complete understanding would be reached. The next turn in the road would lead me to studying the hormones secreted by the brain, not just the thyroid or adrenal glands. The brain, of course, is only a step away from the mind.

One day at a routine staff meeting my supervisor quizzed me on a technical detail in front of the group:

"How many milligrams of iodine did Milne and Greer inject into the rats in their 1959 paper?"

This referred to some seminal experimental work, but I answered offhandedly, because he didn't really want the information, only to put me on the spot. "Maybe two-point-one milligrams. I'll look it up."

"This is something you should have in your head," he barked, irritated.

Everyone in the room grew quiet. I got up, walked over to him, and dumped a bulky file of papers on top of him. "Now you have it in your head," I said, and walked out.

My enraged supervisor followed me into the parking lot. I was agitated, fumbling to start my beat-up Volkswagen Beetle, the signature vehicle of struggling young professionals. He leaned in, speaking with studied control to disguise his anger. "Don't," he warned. "You're throwing away your whole career. I can make that happen."

Which was quite true. The word would go out, and with his disapproval I had no future in endocrinology. But in my mind I wasn't walking away from a career. I was standing up to someone who had tried to humiliate me in front of the group. My impulsive rebellion was instinctive and yet very unlike me.

As it happened, I did wander in the wilderness for a while, but my career wasn't over, because my adviser was so arrogant that he had antagonized a lot of people, one of whom took delight in hiring me if it snubbed my adviser. That part was luck, you might say. Or was I following a hidden path that was working its way forward, apparently at random but actually with complete knowledge of where I needed to go?

In India the right way for a person to go is known as their Dharma, and "right" means that the whole universe is organizing your way forward. To many people this sounds like a mystical idea, and yet all of us can say, at one time or another, that things turned out in an unexpected way beyond our control. The biggest obstacle to finding your Dharma is ego. My blowup could be called a clash of egos, mine against my adviser's. The outcome was that mine got flattened. In an instant I lost a prestigious fellowship and wound up working nights at a suburban ER to support my young family.

There would be many other turning points over the next fifteen years before I found myself immersed in a fascination much deeper than my original one for endocrinology—a fascination with the mind-body connection. The ego stumbles to stay connected to a person's Dharma. You have to learn that your biggest allies along the way are instinct, intuition, staying true to yourself, standing up for your truth, and self-awareness. Your adversaries are naked ambition, blind competitiveness, self-importance, a craving for status, and following second-hand opinions as if they are your truth.

Most people are divided between their allies and their adversaries—I certainly was, and must confess still am, when I find myself in moments of struggle. The ego is a permanent part of the self, and a valuable one. But when it decides to run the show, your inner world becomes distorted. You start to live according to an image you want to protect rather than searching for the connecting thread—the Dharma—that subtly unites every moment of our life. What I learned from my career train wreck was to trust my allies, and as the years passed, one of them—self-awareness—became the ally I could rely on the most, no matter whether I was going through hard times or times of great fulfillment.

This was the story of the one and only Deepak Chopra, MD—founder of the Chopra Foundation, cofounder of the Chopra Center for Wellbeing, and coauthor with Rudolph Tanzi of *Super Brain*, one of many books he has written. His story is very interesting. The universe had different plans for him, and what seemed to be roadblocks were more like detours taking him where he needed to be. Consider all the good Chopra has done and the people he has helped, and he is worth millions. I try to channel this example when things don't go the way I want and trust my self-awareness—my real self, my inner knowing of intuition—to guide me. I have read books, seen videos, and listened to CDs by Chopra, and I find him to be a genius. He has a depth of knowledge about the mind-body connection; he speaks about this in his LinkedIn story and is inspirational. Once we understand how the universe is constructed and operates, we can have anything we want and find true happiness. This all goes back to God or our higher calling, which created the universe in the first place.

Deepak speaks about our self-awareness, which is our spirit, our soul, our essence, our connection to God. This is what we must have faith and trust in to guide us on our journey in life. We should be spiritual beings having a human experience, not human beings having a spiritual experience, according to Dr. Dyer. Being a spiritual being while in human form is an interesting concept, and to achieve this for myself,

I meditate when I can, learn all I can about the mind-body connection, and focus on how it's all connected to the universe. It's a fascinating subject, and scientists are discovering new things every day, many of which I have spoken about. As far as meditation, you don't have to spend hours meditating or going to classes; sometimes just a few minutes a day can help. I sometimes participate in the 21-Day Meditation Experience that Oprah Winfrey and Deepak Chopra have presented. It's very interesting. As I am writing about finding the career for you and living life on purpose, Deepak's story comes to me. Is this a coincidence? I don't think so. There are no coincidences. Just as finding Chopra's story helped me, all falls into place when we're working with the universe.

Quantum physicists tell us that everything breaks down to energy, and Chopra explains that it's not just energy but energy and information. After we break down, the universe to stars and planets and all on earth to the molecular level, then there are atoms, electrons, neutrons, and protons; then there is energy on the quantum level, which breaks down to waveforms with information. This is where quantum physicists study the subatomic particles that make up all material creation. There are studies that say our thoughts, which are made of the same information and energy, are shaping the universe we live in. Winston Churchill said, "We create our universe as we go along." Our thoughts shape the world we live in. When I was younger, my thoughts were limited because my parents' thoughts were limited. They embraced the limiting belief that we were meant to always work and not have much to show for it. That was my belief; I believed only others were more fortunate than us and that we couldn't have the same abundant life they had. Our belief systems are why we are where we are in our lives. It's all about what we are focusing on, and remember that what we focus on expands.

The fascinating aspect of this is particles can only be seen when we observe them according to quantum physicists. When we don't observe the particles, they aren't there or they take on some sort of arbitrary form, like being on autopilot. In the same way, when we take care of a garden, we produce beautiful flowers, but when we neglect the garden, weeds grow. The same is true with our thoughts; if we don't focus on what we want, weeds will grow. This is how we shape our universe. When we focus on what we want with intention, particles start to arrange themselves to produce what we are thinking about. This can be applied to every circumstance. So it's very important to only focus on what we want and keep our thoughts positive. Remember, when we change the way we look at things, those things will start to change, which is quantum physics. It's our thoughts that are producing the energy and information necessary to produce our desires. When I wanted to attract my first high-end car into my life, I focused on it and had the belief, which is very important, that it would come into my life. Then little by little, the universe started to rearrange itself to make it reality. This can be applied to anything in our lives we desire. This is the science that supports the law of attraction, which I want to explain so you can have a better understanding of how it works. Even if you don't understand it, as long as you have faith, trust, belief, and intention, it will be enough.

How does all this coincide with finding your career? If we are focusing on finding the right career for us, then we are attracting that career into our lives using the law of attraction.

This is how the universe shapes itself for us, and it's doing this by arranging the particles that I spoke about. *The Secret* talks about how we are spiritual energy beings operating in a larger spiritual energy field. If we give this some thought, it just makes sense that whatever we think about will shape the world we live in; our attention will make it so. We not only shape our world but also the world around us. If we have good thoughts, not only will we benefit, but everyone else will too. Consider past inventors, whose inventions contributed to making a better life for all of us. If we look at electricity and communication technology, we see how many products using these technologies make our lives more enjoyable and easier. Because of these technologies, we have all the multimedia that entertains and keep us informed and the communication devices that keep us connected. The list goes on and on. There is no limit to what we can now achieve; the possibilities are endless for everyone, not just the inventors.

We can achieve anything. We all start out the same. Some do have an advantage from a young age, but many who have achieved greatness started out with nothing. There are so many stories of people who started out with nothing and now are rich and famous, living fulfilled, enjoyable lives. We live in a world of all possibilities; anything is possible. I can't say this enough.

CHAPTER 14

THE CAREER SEARCH

Many things can motivate us to pursue different careers, and money is always a thought. Most of us think about making enough money to sustain themselves and their family. However, money is not the only thing we should be thinking about when deciding what we want to do for the rest of our lives. What we gain from our careers should be well-rounded; the benefits should include fulfillment, advancement, enjoyment, excitement, inspiration, and challenge to give us opportunities to improve upon on ourselves. If we acquire these things, then money will flow. Choosing a career that offers these benefits will ensure you have a job you want to go to every day. Most of us dread going to the same, sometimes boring job. If the hours on the clock stand still, if you have a hard time getting up for work and feel you are going through the motions day by day, that is an indication you are not in the career for you. When I first started working, the days seemed to go by slowly. And most of my jobs were just that—a job. I had no idea I should be in a position that was inspiring and challenging. We usually look for a career that has some sort of advancement and reward, but we must also look at ourselves and find our passion. What is it we want to do? What is calling us? What makes us happy?

Sometimes we get stuck in a position we had to take, our career takes a downturn, or we just lose interest. That doesn't mean we have to stay where we're at or stay in the same position for the rest of our lives. Also, it doesn't mean we have to go back to school for many years to get a degree or a different one. When I was younger, a good friend of mine gave me a set of cassettes tapes called *The Physiology of Achievement*. In it was a story called the "Acres of Diamonds." It was a very inspiring story that demonstrated how we don't have to be stuck in a job or career. Here is that story:

> The Acres of Diamonds story—a true one—is told of an African farmer who heard tales about other farmers who had made millions by discovering diamond mines. These tales so excited the farmer that he could hardly wait to sell his farm and go prospecting for diamonds himself. He sold the farm and spent the rest of his life wandering the African continent searching unsuccessfully for the gleaming gems that brought such high prices on the markets of the world. Finally, worn out and in a fit of despondency, he threw himself into a river and drowned.
>
> Meanwhile, the man who had bought his farm happened to be crossing the small stream on the property one day, when suddenly there was a bright flash of blue and red light from the stream bottom. He bent down and picked up a

stone. It was a good-sized stone, and admiring it, he brought it home and put it on his fireplace mantel as an interesting curiosity.

Several weeks later a visitor picked up the stone, looked closely at it, hefted it in his hand, and nearly fainted. He asked the farmer if he knew what he'd found. When the farmer said, no, that he thought it was a piece of crystal, the visitor told him he had found one of the largest diamonds ever discovered. The farmer had trouble believing that. He told the man that his creek was full of such stones, not all as large as the one on the mantel, but sprinkled generously throughout the creek bottom.

The farm the first farmer had sold, so that he might find a diamond mine, turned out to be one of the most productive diamond mines on the entire African continent. The first farmer had owned, free and clear ... acres of diamonds. But he had sold them for practically nothing, in order to look for them elsewhere. The moral is clear: If the first farmer had only taken the time to study and prepare himself to learn what diamonds looked like in their rough state, and to thoroughly explore the property he had before looking elsewhere, all his wildest dreams would have come true.

The thing about this story that has so profoundly affected millions of people is the idea that each of us is, at this very moment, standing in the middle of our own acres of diamonds. If we had only had the wisdom and patience to intelligently and effectively explore the work in which we're now engaged, to explore ourselves, we would most likely find the riches we seek, whether they be financial or intangible or both.

After the story, they go on to speak about a man who owned a gas station in Arizona. One day, as he was pumping gas for a customer, he realized the customer had money in his pocket he would spend if there were other items available. The gas station owner then started to offer other items, and his business started to grow. He offered everything from candy to fishing boats and trailers. The moral of the story is, if we feel stuck in our present position, we shouldn't just throw it all away and go for something else immediately. We need to first evaluate our present circumstance, and I would suggest looking at our self from afar. I explained the importance of observing ourselves objectively, as if we were looking at someone else, in the relationships section. Look to see what is going on around you; look for opportunities in your present field that intrigue and interest you. There may be a position in another department at your present place of employment or elsewhere. You may discover more training is needed, but that doesn't mean you have to go back to school for another degree. Sometimes just taking a few classes or going for a certificate will be sufficient. The main thing is, you must pursue something you are passionate about. It should attract you and make you feel inspired. It should be something you could do all day, and the hours on the clock will fly by. Treat yourself like you're your own business, always learning and growing about the field you are in. If you do all this and are passionate and inspired, then it won't even feel like work. That is the beauty of following your destiny or dharma.

The following is a quote from *The Secret*: "Be aware of the big difference between inspired action and activity. Activity comes from the brain-mind and is rooted in disbelief and lack of faith—you are taking action to "make" your desire happen. Inspired action is allowing the law to work through you and to move you. Activity feels hard. Inspired action feels wonderful."

When I first heard the acres of diamonds story, I was very inspired. At the time, I was searching for something other than what I was doing. I did take some additional classes, and then I stopped when I wanted to try a career in sales. At the time, I was working for a government contractor that was going out of business and later did close. I knew I had to move on and wanted to try sales. Well, sales, unfortunately, was not for me, and I found myself out of work. I went through several different positions back in my field of technology, what I knew best, CAD (computer aided design). I found several positions with employers in New York City, one of which let me go two months before my wedding due to cutbacks and another company that is no longer around. Luckily, after my wedding, I did find a couple of positions that paid enough to sustain a home and family. One of my positions was with the Port Authority of New York and New Jersey at One World Trade Center on the 72nd floor. At the time, I worked as a consultant. I wanted a direct position with benefits to be employed by the Port Authority. I was still a CAD operator, and I was starting to move to IT (information technology), a career I had wanted to pursue for some time. All these jobs were just that: jobs. And I was starting to realize that IT was my passion.

Meanwhile, my supervisor informed me I needed to go back to school for more training, or there would not be a position for me in the future. Reluctantly, I went back to school for my bachelor's degree. It was either that or no job, and I had a house to pay for and a wife and baby to support. I went back to college at night at my expense. My wife was also working, and she had to drop off and pick up our daughter from the babysitter. She had to work because her job provided health benefits, and since I was a consultant, I had none. My commute to the city was three to four hours a day. With that and my regular workday, plus overtime, I was putting in a lot of hours. The money was good, but with all the expenses of the house, the commute, child care, and school, we were just getting by. The days were long, and we were always rushing around with all we had to do. Between all that was going on and focusing on the day-to-day responsibilities of being new parents, it was hard to remember the acres of diamonds story.

Going to school put me in a different mind-set and a higher frequency. I started to get involved in IT at my job. Eventually, I received a position in the field I wanted as a LAN administrator consulting for Lockheed Martin and assigned to the FAA. Working for Lockheed Martin, I received health benefits and tuition reimbursement, which was extremely important, since I was attending school at night. My place of employment was also out of the city and closer to my home, another great advantage. This enabled me to continue school at no expense to me and work in the field I wanted, and my wife could quit her job, which she hated because her responsibilities had changed for the worse. She was very happy to be able to stay home with our daughter, and the plan was for her to babysit other children so we could make ends meet. Unfortunately, she was only able to find one child to watch. And even with the pay from my job and what my wife was being paid, we were facing financial difficulties. Luckily, we had money in the bank, but you can only draw on savings for so long.

Even though my salary wasn't enough, I knew I was in the right field, and I knew things would get better. My immediate supervisor suggested I stop taking college classes and pursue certification as a CNE (Certified Novell Engineer), which would most benefit my present position. I followed this advice, and a year later, I was a CNE. My immediate supervisor moved to another department in the organization, and I was given his responsibilities. I was learning so much so fast; it was like going to school all day and all night. With all I had learned and the added responsibilities, I was not being compensated in terms of salary. So I started to look for another position.

The strange thing is, nine months after I started my position with the FAA, my wife saw an ad in the paper for an IT position with Nassau BOCES (Board of Cooperative Educational Services). I applied for the position. I needed to take a civil service exam, which I did. After two exams, five interviews, and two years, I was offered the position. I was ecstatic; with the position came room for advancement and everything I was looking for. I am a huge believer in education, and what better way to follow my passion than to work for an educational agency that oversaw fifty-six school districts. I was raised by parents who did not value education, and once I realized how important education is, I became an advocate for it. I now know that education is key. Combined with our abilities, talents, and our passion, education helps ensure there is nothing we can't achieve. This position has sustained me and my family. In addition, it's been rewarding and challenging. I have learned and accomplished things I never thought I could. I was brought up to believe I could never accomplish great things, and due to all the negative thinking I was exposed to, I had once embraced that belief. I had succumbed to the notion that good things happened to other people. This was my parents' belief, and of course, their memes trickled down to me.

I share this part of my life because of the chain of events that transpired. Throughout this whole episode, my thoughts and prayers were on achieving a position close to where I lived, with benefits, room for advancement, and a high enough salary to sustain my family. Finally, after all the prayers and candles I lit, it happened. The reason it took so long was that doubts entered my mind and negativity was a part of my thinking. The universe had to take me through the lessons I needed to achieve my desire.

The other interesting thing is, when I was working at the Port Authority, I wanted to be hired as a permanent employee. Even after the building I worked in was bombed in 1993, I still wanted to work; I believed I would find opportunities with the Port Authority. Then in 2001, we all know what happened; on September 11, many people who worked in the building I'd once worked in lost their lives in a horrific tragedy. A current coworker of mine was working in the building during the 9/11 tragedy but was on maternity leave. Everyone on the floor she worked with perished, and she could not go back. Now she works in my building at Nassau BOCES. Her children saved her life, and now she can continue to enjoy her family, and I can enjoy mine. For some reason, God did not want me there; He had other plans for me. In 2001, my children were very young, and I could not imagine them growing up without a father. Nor can I imagine my wife having to cope by herself.

All these events enabled me to be where I am today. All the different jobs, the times I was out of work, the additional classes I needed to take, and the experience of working in the city led me to having a good job in a field I enjoy. These experiences taught me the lessons I needed to learn to bring me to this point. Being in information technology, I was able to work at it all day and even at night if I had to. The hours would just fly by. I really enjoyed learning as much as I could, and there is plenty to learn. Helping people with their issues gave me a feeling of fulfillment. Even though I had to go through all these experiences, there was always a choice. I didn't have to take a job in the city, go to therapy, or go back to school. I didn't have to get married and have children. But I'm glad I did all this. Without my career and my family, where would I be now? Possibly in a dead-end job, alone, miserable, and always wondering what if and what went wrong. The universe or God sent me the lessons I needed to learn in order to achieve all I wanted. Even though I still had doubts, I just kept the faith.

I've hear religious people say God answers all prayers, and for the most part, everything I prayed for came to fruition. When I was young and a huge New York Yankees fan, I used to pray the team would win the World Series. Back in the '60s, the Yankees were losing most of their games. Then eventually, they started winning many World Series and became a very strong ball club. I was just a little kid praying my team would win; that's all. Was it coincidence? Or were my prayers really answered? It took years for this to happen, but so did many other things I prayed for. A wife, a career, a house, children, and the list goes on and on—getting them took time.

The Secret says that when we pray, we should pray as if we already have what we are praying for. In Mark 11:24, we read, "Therefore I say unto you, What things soever ye desire, when ye pray, believe that ye receive *them*, and ye shall have *them*" (King James Bible). Praying as if you will, indeed, receive what you desire shows you have faith and confidence in the universe. And it puts you on the frequency of receiving. That's the frequency we need to be on if we want to receive what we want. *The Secret* says we should *ask*, *believe*, and *receive*. Ask the universe for what we want, believe we are receiving, and then feel as we would feel once we receive what we are asking for. If what we want is in line with what the universe wants for us, it will just flow. This is what I mean when I say that through doing God's work, being in line with the universe, and utilizing our abilities, we will attain the abundance, joy, and fulfillment we are seeking and deserve.

CHAPTER 15

GOALS, MOTIVATION, AND INSPIRATION

It's always good to have goals that motivate us into action. Earlier, I mentioned Brian Tracy's definition of happiness as "the progressive realization of a worthy goal." As we work on our goals, we start to see results; the more results we see, the more motivated we get. Results and motivation bring us a feeling of fulfillment and achievement. Then we become proud and say to ourselves, *Look at what I can do*! This in turn brings us a feeling of happiness. It's okay to be proud of ourselves and see our accomplishments. Just don't become a show-off or get cocky, because no one likes that. As long as we are content with and confident in ourselves and our abilities, we don't need to rub our successes in others' faces. Others will see your worth and, in time, will send you compliments. You just need to be patient.

We should always set goals and challenge ourselves to be better and to evolve. Motivation is great. However, being inspired is much better because it gives us a sense of God-Realization (an ability to see things from a spiritual perspective like God does), as Dr. Dyer explains in *Inspiration*. There is a difference between motivation and inspiration. Motivation is when we get an idea, set goals, and do our best to stay on task no matter what. But inspiration, being in-spirit, is when an idea gets ahold of us and takes us where we are destined to be. Inspiration puts us in spirit and is connected to God or the universe. It is our true selves coming out and telling us this is something we must do. It was like that for me with my career in information technology. I just had this knowing that IT was right for me, almost as if it were a calling. I trusted my inner self, and that gave me great fulfillment. I was able to totally immerse myself in a career that both inspired me and supported my family.

When we focus intently on helping people, the universe will give us whatever we need. Perhaps you are asking yourself, How am I going to get a job, get married, and support a family? We need to have faith in God. He will give us all we need. One of my wife's cousins said this to me right after my wife and I had married and were thinking of having children. I was scared and had no clue how we were going to do it. That was over twenty years ago, and I remember his advice like yesterday. And, yes, he was right. Dr. Dyer says the same thing. The universe gives you all you need as you approach source, and for me, the proof comes in the form of personal experience.

This brings me to the next topic—our abilities. I have heard and read "The Parable of the Three Servants," found in Matthew 25:14–30 (New Living Translation) many times, and now I understand it. First, let me share the parable, and then I'll explain:

> Again, the Kingdom of Heaven can be illustrated
> by the story of a man going on a long trip. He

called together his servants and entrusted his money to them while he was gone. He gave five bags of silver to one, two bags of silver to another, and one bag of silver to the last—dividing it in proportion to their abilities. He then left on his trip.

The servant who received the five bags of silver began to invest the money and earned five more. The servant with two bags of silver also went to work and earned two more. But the servant who received the one bag of silver dug a hole in the ground and hid the master's money.

After a long time their master returned from his trip and called them to give an account of how they had used his money. The servant to whom he had entrusted the five bags of silver came forward with five more and said, "Master, you gave me five bags of silver to invest, and I have earned five more."

The master was full of praise. "Well done, my good and faithful servant. You have been faithful in handling this small amount, so now I will give you many more responsibilities. Let's celebrate together!"

The servant who had received the two bags of silver came forward and said, "Master, you gave me two bags of silver to invest, and I have earned two more."

The master said, "Well done, my good and faithful servant. You have been faithful in handling this small amount, so now I will give you many more responsibilities. Let's celebrate together!"

Then the servant with the one bag of silver came and said, "Master, I knew you were a harsh man, harvesting crops you didn't plant and gathering crops you didn't cultivate. I was afraid I would lose your money, so I hid it in the earth. Look, here is your money back."

But the master replied, "You wicked and lazy servant! If you knew I harvested crops I didn't plant and gathered crops I didn't cultivate, why didn't you deposit my money in the bank? At least I could have gotten some interest on it."

Then he ordered, "Take the money from this servant, and give it to the one with the ten bags of silver. To those who use well what they are given, even more will be given, and they will have an abundance. But from those who do nothing, even what little they have will be taken away. Now throw this useless servant into outer darkness, where there will be weeping and gnashing of teeth."

In this parable, we have the master and three servants with their silver. There are several interpretations of this passage, but I will explain what it means to me after all the research I have done. The parable explains that we are given talents and that how we use them will determine our place in heaven. Ultimately, that is true; how we conduct ourselves in this life determines our next. This is what I have been talking about when I say that we must do God's work. God gave us special abilities and talents to develop for the benefit of all. We are here to grow, evolve, help others, and be happy and fulfilled. The same things parents want for their children, God wants for us also. By doing what we love to do and helping others, we are doing God's work, establishing a place for us in the next life, and loving the process.

God gives us not bags of silver but different talents and abilities. It's up to us to identify, embrace, and refine what God has given us. Just like in the story about the acres of diamonds, sometimes we can't know what we have until we start to look around. We must search and investigate in order to see what was given to us. The first two servants took what they had, invested, and doubled it, and the master said to them, "Well done, my good and faithful servant. You have been faithful in handling this small amount, so now I will give you many more responsibilities." The key here is that the master says the servant was faithful in handling what he was given, which means the servant had faith in his ability or talents and applied them to the fullest. Then the master says he will give the servant many more responsibilities. Since the servant realizes his newfound abilities and talents, he will now expand upon them and continue to grow and evolve to his full potential and fulfill his purpose. The third servant was scared to invest the silver his master gave him, fearing his master would be angry if he lost it. The servant focused on the fear and brought it into fruition. The master was not angry and disappointed that the servant didn't invest the silver. He was angry and disappointed that the servant was afraid to invest the silver; he knew the servant had the potential to achieve more but was afraid to.

This is what happens to many of us. We get scared to embrace certain abilities; we are afraid of failing; or we feel some goals are beyond our reach. Sometimes we have burning desires, but we may have to go back to school or take some additional training. We tells ourselves that achieving our dreams will take too many years—that by then, we will be years older. The question you have to ask yourself is simple: how old will I be if I don't do it? The answer is the same age. Whether something takes you one year or ten years to accomplish, you will still be one or ten years older, whether you do it or not. We can come up with many excuses for not embracing our burning desires. *It will be hard. I don't have time. I have too many other responsibilities. I'm too tired. I'm not smart enough.* The list can go on and on. The most important thing you need to remember, which I have mentioned many times, is that if you are living in line with what the universe or God wants for you, what you're doing will just flow, as if moving with current of a fast-moving river. This will bring you all the inspiration you need, will fulfill your burning desires, and will bring joy and happiness into your life. It was like that for me with information technology. I had a burning desire for it, and when my manager at the port authority told me I needed to go back to school, I got on the right frequency. I started a process of learning that in turn initiated the chain of events that led me to my IT classes and, eventually, to a successful career. The universe guided me in the direction I needed to go. My desires moved me forward.

Billy Crystal performed a show on HBO called *700 Sundays*, which was very funny and inspiring. He told his story of growing up with his father for the 700 Sundays he had with him until his father passed when Billy was only fifteen. Billy enjoyed his

Sundays with his father; that was the only day his father was home, and the two had a very good relationship. Billy was devastated when his father passed, and he struggled with the fallout of his father's death for years. He talks about being on his high school basketball team. Billy wasn't a strong player, but there was one shot he had to take for the championship game. He hesitated, and then he heard his mother yell, "Billy just go for it!" Ever since then, that's what he did—he just went for it. His mother supported him and gave him inspiration, and of course, he has been very successful. This is what he speaks about in *700 Sundays*. So I say the same thing to, I take his advice myself— just go for it. Who knows? Maybe it's God speaking to you.

Matthew 25:29 (New Living Translation) says, "To those who use well what they are given, even more will be given, and they will have an abundance. But from those who do nothing, even what little they have will be taken away." This means that as we develop our talents, we will gain the experience we need to fulfill our desires. And the more we use them, the stronger they will be. If we don't embrace our talents, what we have will fade away. It's like when we exercise. The more we do it, the better results we get. And if we let ourselves go, well, you know what happens. So stop wasting your life away watching TV, playing video or electronic games, and texting everyone about nonsense. Find your desire and run with it. If one of your desires is within the aforementioned categories, then embrace it. If you love TV and know all the players, become a movie critic or look for opportunities in that field. If you love video or electronic games, find opportunities there. Gaming is a very large field today; the gaming industry has made many advances in computer graphics and technology.

In the book of Matthew, New International Version, we find the following passages. Matthew 5:3, "Blessed are the poor in spirit, for theirs is the kingdom of heaven." and Matthew 5:5, "Blessed are the meek, for they will inherit the earth." Once again, there are several interpretations of this. These passages speak about those who are poor in spirit and need God's help, while others who are rich do not seem to need God's help. Sometimes we see people who seem to have it all. They have high levels of self-esteem, and are sure of themselves. These are good traits to have. However, they miss the point that all good comes from God. They are not thankful to the universe for their good fortune, and when things go wrong, they have a very difficult time coping. Those who are called "poor in spirit" may feel down on themselves, have lower levels of self-esteem, be unsure, and always look to God for help. When things do get better, they are thankful and realize all good comes from God. So those who are poor in spirit and experiencing difficult times are driven to better themselves by looking to God and their true selves, which is also a part of God. This puts them in a state of God-Realization, and they find themselves following the flow that will move them toward fulfilling their destiny.

Every time we are faced with difficult times and we get down on ourselves, we find ourselves poor in spirit. We look to a higher calling for help. I say, don't despair; if we ask for help, the universe will guide us through the events and lessons we need to experience to get to a better place. This is what I have been talking about throughout this book. Ask the universe or God for help, and we will be guided to the place we want to be and should be. When we are faced with a disaster or difficult time, these events propel us forward to a better place, with more knowledge, understanding, empathy, peace, faith, and love. Love is the strongest emotion, and when we are faced with hard times or even health issues, we should send love to the event with faith and expect the best possible outcome. Why love and faith? Love is the strongest emotion and the one that brings us closest to God; it vibrates on the highest frequency. And when this is combined with faith, there is nothing we cannot achieve. In the quantum world, this is the most powerful signal we can send out to the universe.

Let me explain further. We cannot have a universe without mind entering into it. The big bang was created by God (all the loving energy in the universe) and thought (the mind of God). Together, God and thought created what we know as the universe today, and it's still expanding. This can work for us as well. We have the energy and the thought because we are part of universal energy and we have a mind to think. Not only do we have energy; our energy is part of God. Since God is connected to everything, so are we; and everything is connected on the quantum level. In Dr. Dyer's "The Secrets of an Inspirational (In-Spirit) Life" audio CDs, he speaks about Jesus telling us, "We can all do the things that He has done and more." If we think about this and the knowledge that we are all connected to the universe's loving energy, then it all seems to fall into place. I found the following, by Pastor Jim Feeney, PhD, online:

Imagine yourself healing the sick, raising the dead, cleansing the lepers, or casting out demons! Jesus Christ said that you can do these things and more. Based on what? On faith, on believing in Him. If you can believe, you too can do the mighty works that Jesus did. He Himself has promised you this!

John 14:12 (KJV), "Verily, verily, I say unto you, He that believeth on me, the works that I do shall he do also; and greater works than these shall he do; because I go unto my Father."

This is a plain-language promise from Jesus Himself: if you believe on Him, you can do the works that He did. Why? How could they? How could we? Because of our faith in Jesus and His unfailing promises.

How does this relate to us and to quantum physics? There are people today who say they can heal others, and there are stories of people healing themselves from fatal illnesses and injuries. There are even stories of people performing different types of miracles. When our mind, true self, or energy connects with universal energy with 100 percent faith, we receive unlimited power to manifest our intention. I believe this is the same process Jesus used to perform His miracles. Quantum physicists explain that once we have an intention and focus on it, our thoughts produce the energy and information to start to produce the arrangement of particles with the same energy and information we desire to manifest. Particles are only there when we observe them, putting our attention on them with our intention. That's why it is important to keep our attention focused on what we want and not on what we don't want because the latter will also manifest. Putting our attention on our worries or negative thoughts brings more of that into our lives with the same process. This is what *The Secret* explains in terms of the law of attraction.

So, is all this religion, science, or magic? It's all the same—religion is science; magic is science. Put it all together, and you have miracles. Consider all the miracles Jesus performed. Were they magic, religion, or science? I believe it all breaks down to science. If God created all things, He also created the atoms, molecules, and all the science that goes with it. We are still learning and discovering new things every day. Certain inventions and technologies exist today that make things considered inconceivable years ago not only possible but mundane; now that we understand the science behind all the inventions and technologies, not only do we use it— we accept it. There are still so many things to discover and invent, and any one of us—and I mean *any* one *of us*—can be a pioneer or inventor. It doesn't matter how much education we have or don't have; we all have this ability. We just need to have the thought and the intention, and if we keep to that, we will eventually achieve our desires. The most important ingredient is faith; through it, we must banish all doubt!

CHAPTER 16

BALANCING CAREER
AND SPIRITUALITY

Careers can be very important; we can become very successful and wealthy. Many may feel that being rich is not spiritual. According to Catherine Ponder—who is featured in *The Secret* for her Millionaires of the Bible series—that cannot be further from the truth. Ponder is a spiritual writer who speaks about how Jesus, Moses, Jacob, and others of the Bible were not only spiritual teachers but also millionaires. They lived very affluent lifestyles, even more so than some of the millionaires of today. If you think about it, it only makes sense that being rich would go hand in hand with spirituality. When we are very spiritual, like I have become, we just want to help people in need. There are many ways to help others. You can join the Peace Corps, visit people who are ill, give your time to worthy causes, and on and on. These are all admirable choices, but just think how much more you could help others if you were wealthy.

I know that whenever I am doing well and have extra money to give to my family, friends, and others, it just feels great. I would gladly give to charities, give extra tips to people who deserve it, contribute extra to family functions, and buy my children the things they wanted. However, I had to be careful not to spoil them and be sure they were grateful for all they had. I always gave what I could. I appreciated and was very grateful to be able to do this because this was not always the case for me. There is nothing like taking your children to Disney World and seeing them have a great time and being thankful for it. What a fantastic feeling!

Some people believe that money makes you bad. When all you think about is money, it will start to consume you. Money in itself, though, doesn't make you bad; it's the attachment to money that makes you bad. When people make money and it becomes their god and all they think about, that becomes an issue. In Mark 10:25 (New American Standard Bible), we read, "It is easier for a camel to go through the eye of a needle than for a rich man to enter the kingdom of God." We come into the world with nothing, and we leave the world with nothing. No amount of material items we accumulate means anything to us when we die. You can still be rich and go to heaven; you just have to be detached from the money and realize money is just a tool to help you and others in this life. We should not put a price tag on anything. We shouldn't tell other people that we drive a car worth x amount of dollars or brag about the value or cost of our home. What we can afford or not afford should have no bearing on who or what we are. We are all part of the same energy field; we are all equal, a part of God.

Money doesn't make you bad. What matters is how you use it. Money puts a roof over your head and food on the table. It heats and cools your home. And it educates people so they can contribute to society and sustain themselves. Money can be used for so many good things, and it can help others. According to Deepak Chopra, when all you think about is money and how much you have in the bank, you are really poor. By being attached to it, you give all your energy to it. Instead, we must be attached to ourselves, to our true selves. Chopra explains this as *youthful vigor*. He says, "We experience health when our identity of who we are comes from reference to the self. When we identify with objects, whether they are situations, circumstances, people, or things, then we relinquish our energy to the object of reference. As a result, we feel lack of energy and vitality. When our identity comes from the self, then we keep our energy to ourselves. We feel energetic, we feel powerful, and we experience youthful vigor."

As long as we don't attach ourselves to money or an object, then our energy will come from our true selves and won't be absorbed by the object. When I was young, I used to put all my energy into my car, as many young men do. I always tried to have a nice car. And I'd think, *Look at my car. Look at what I have.* Boy, was I wrong. Instead of putting my energy and whole true self into my car, I should have been looking within to my true self. People should see my true self, not what I have. As I have gotten older, and hopefully wiser, I have come to realize that any material item I have is not a part of me; the item is only what it is. If someone says to me, "Nice car" or compliments some other object, such as my jacket or phone, I say something like, "Yes, it is," or "I like it," or "I enjoy it." It's not a compliment to me. The object is just what it is—an object—and I have no attachment to it.

So I say this: Go and find the career for you. Follow your passion, your deepest desires. Ask the universe or God for guidance and direction. Go and make your fortune and *know* that your fortune is just that—some*thing* you share with your family, friends, and the world. As long as you have it, spend it. Give it. Money must flow and circulate like blood. It belongs to everyone, and the more you give, the more will come back. Just have faith. Never put money before anyone, because karma is a bitch, and you can't hide from it. As long as you follow these basic principles, all will fall into place.

My wish for you and for all of us is that we all find what we are looking for—true happiness. I hope that we all flow with everyone and the universe, that we are connected, and that we don't fight, but rather, accept what comes into our lives and learn from it. Sometimes people start on a journey of improving their lives, things start to get better and then after a short time say that nothing is going right. They find themselves in a bad situation or place. It feels horrible but it's most likely the universe sending the detour needed to give them divine guidance. This has happened to many people, and I am of course included among them. According to Catherine Ponder, this is called "chemicalization." Ponder describes this process in an essay called "Chemicalization: A Cleansing, Healing Process" as follows:

> Recently a civil service employee in a distant city said, "I have your book, *The Dynamic Laws of Prosperity*, and it is the best book on the subject I have ever read. For a time, I worked with the laws you described and they brought dynamic good into my life. But suddenly, I am frightened and discouraged. The last few weeks,

everything seems to have gone in reverse. What has happened?"

That lady was relieved to learn that another dynamic law was working for her—the law of chemicalization.

You've heard it said that things have to get worse sometimes before they can get better; that the getting worse process is actually a part of the improvement process; that what seems failure is actually success being born in the situation. That's chemicalization!

Chemicalization sounds like a negative process, but actually it is a very positive one, a natural, normal one. Though it is an uncomfortable experience, it is worth going through, because it is always a sign that cleansing is taking place. Something higher and better always results from this experience.

When these periods come, remind yourself, "This is nothing to fear. This is not evil. There is only good at work in this experience. Healing is now taking place in my world. I rest, relax and let it." As you nonresistantly meet chemicalization in this way, very soon brighter conditions will appear.

Emmet Fox, who was a New Thought spiritual leader of the early 20th century, famous for his large Divine Science church services held in New York City during the Great Depression, has described the healing process of chemicalization:

It seems as though everything begins to go wrong at once. This may be disconcerting, but it is really a good sign. Suppose your whole world seems to rock on its foundation. Hold on steadily, and let it rock, and when the rocking is over, the picture will have reassembled itself into something much nearer to your heart's desire.

Chemicalization means that things are coming out in a better state of affairs than ever before. Regardless of what seems to be happening, it never means anything else. When a physical or mental disturbance arises after your deliberate use of right thinking, it is always a sign that your right thinking is at work clearing out the negative, so that the positive power of good can gain complete dominion of your world.

As you practice the prosperity laws given in my books, faithfully writing out your desires, making a wheel of fortune, commanding your good to appear, creating a master plan for success, and as you practice the healing laws faithfully invoking denial, forgiveness, release, and affirmations of love, praise, etc.—don't be surprised if your world begins to rock!

When it does say to yourself, "This is good! Those laws are working for me in a dynamic way. Only dynamic good shall come from this cleansing experience." You are having a mental, emotional, and perhaps even a physical "spring cleaning." How free, unburdened, and ready for better health and greater health and greater good you will be as this cleansing perfects you and your world.

There have been many times in my life when I felt nothing was going right. During these times, I have felt like an absolute failure in all areas of my life, and I drudged through it. I never thought I would get over my skin condition, meet someone compatible who would love me, have children, or find a job close to home that would sustain me and my family. I went through so many events that I never thought I would overcome, especially given my negative upbringing. My parents always painted a gloomy picture of life, and of course their belief system became mine. As I went through the difficult experiences in my life, I learned lessons and encountered experiences that were necessities on my path. I knew in the back of my mind that life could be better. All these lessons and experiences taught me how to reach for my full potential, follow my life's purpose, and be on a "mission from God."

I have shared here my life and all the challenges I had to overcome with money, relationships, health, and career. I never gave up. Deep down I always knew there was a better life, and God was, and still is, always there with me. All the negative experiences in my life led me on a journey of discovery and enlightenment. Many things came to me because my thoughts were on having a better life, even though I didn't realize the connection at the time. To this day, I continue to learn, grow, and evolve. I am constantly seeking to improve my life and the lives of others with all I have learned as I continue my journey on this earth. With all I have encountered and experienced, I feel ageless. I believe I can accomplish anything, regardless of where I am in my life. I accept what comes, whether good or bad, as a learning process. When someone asks me to do something or I am invited to a function, I try to always say yes. I do give it some thought, however. I consider whether it is a positive event, where I can help, or whether it can help me. And if it is fun, even better. We live in a universe of all possibilities. We can have anything we want, as long as we are in line with source, know who we are (are coming from our true selves), and are passionate and filled with love and understanding.

I try to focus on bringing abundance into my life; being nonjudgmental; excluding no one; forgiving everyone, especially myself; and letting negative events go. I remember that the gift of health is keeping me alive, and I focus on being in a state that will allow me to receive the goodness life has to offer. I remember too that my thoughts create my world as I go along. We are all connected through the loving energy of the universe, and we all have a divine purpose. We owe it to ourselves and to others to discover what our unique divine purposes are on our journeys through this life. By doing this, we can make this world a better place for everyone, including the people on the other side of the planet and ourselves.

I thank God every day with the following because, even if we don't have something yet, we should thank it into our lives:

- Thank you for today and every day.
- Thank you for my continued growth with my job, career, spirituality, humanity, and talents so I can live life on purpose.

- Thank you for knowing which talents to develop further so I can be inspired, confident, and in line with my divine purpose.
- Thank you for my continued growth with my immediate and extended family.
- Thank you for helping my faith, hope, belief, and trust grow and banish all the doubt with knowing and confidence.
- Thank you for guiding me through the challenges I face every day and for giving me the grace, wisdom, and confidence to overcome them.
- Thank you for helping me deal with difficult people and become a better person.
- Thank you for peace of mind and financial freedom.
- Thank you for making me an instrument of high levels of positive energy, creativity, intelligence, well-being, abundance, peace, and love, which flows through me from heaven. Amen!

This is how it is explained in *The Secret* and in the Bible (Mark 11:24, King James Bible): "Therefore I say unto you, What things soever ye desire, when ye pray, believe that ye receive *them*, and ye shall have *them*." This is one the most important fundamentals we need to keep in mind. If we feel we already have what we desire and are thankful for it, whatever we desire and are grateful for will come into our lives sooner than later. And sometimes we will receive even more than we anticipated. So be thankful, and receive all the good you deserve.

God bless!